COLERIDGE THE POET

# Coleridge the Poet

by George Watson

*London*
Routledge and Kegan Paul

First published 1966
by Routledge and Kegan Paul Ltd
Broadway House, 68-74 Carter Lane
London E.C.4

Printed in Great Britain
by Northumberland Press Limited
Gateshead

*To Donald Davie*

'The practice of an art
is to convert all terms
into the terms of art.'

# Contents

# Preface

This book arose naturally out of another, *The Literary Critics* (1962); but the connection is hardly obvious, and a word of explanation may be in order. In the earlier work, which was a history of descriptive criticism in English since Dryden, I tried to show by examples how little resemblance to the facts of literary history one common view of the interrelationship between literature and criticism bears. I mean the view that literature is about life, and that criticism is about literature—so that criticism does duty at the best as a poor relation, being about life at two removes. This view has such a commonsensical air about it, and is believed by so many who have no reason to believe in anything except because they think it true, that I might decently have hesitated even longer before opposing it openly. In fact I have chosen to work through specific cases: first, by showing that the relationship between the poetic activity and the critical in poets like Dryden, Johnson, Coleridge, Arnold and Eliot was more intimate and continuous than the common view would suggest; and now, in a more searching view of Coleridge alone, by attempting to show how little substance there has ever been in the myth of his defeat or abdication as a poet —to reveal, in fact, how successful a poet he was, and how critical a poet; how partial and inaccurate the assumption, in such a case, that literature can only usefully be about life; and how critical the act of creation itself may be.

In dealing with secondary sources I have adopted a solution which is already familiar in an age of thriving literary studies, and likely to become more so: I have concentrated most of my discussion of other works in a first chapter, which is a summary review of Coleridge studies from the standpoint of one who thinks the defeatist view of his poetic achievement to have been overstated. For the rest of the book, and especially in the later chapters on individual poems, I have not usually referred to the views of others unless for some special purpose, but simply followed my own argument and given references only to direct quotations. I have silently accepted the traditional dating of 'Christabel', for example, and the attribution of 'The Mad Monk' to Coleridge rather than to Wordsworth, because the contrary arguments have so far failed to convince me. To behave in this way is to risk charges of ignorance, or plagiarism, or both. I should find ignorance an accusation hard enough to rebut, and remain deeply conscious of how much in romantic studies, in spite of my best efforts, I may have missed. Plagiarism would be a graver matter; at all events, I am conscious of many debts. James Dykes Campbell's edition of the *Poetical Works* (1893) contains what is still the best commentary to the poems. The books and articles of Humphry House, Kathleen Coburn, J. B. Beer and George Whalley have taught me much, and their friendship more; and the Bollingen Foundation has earned the gratitude of every scholar in the field by sponsoring the first complete edition of the notebooks. The encouragement of Cambridge colleagues, notably Miss Barbara Everett, Professor Graham Hough, Mr A. G. Lee and Dr David Frost, has been indispensable to me. And my debt to the editors of the following works will be evident on every page.

## ABBREVIATIONS OF COLERIDGE'S WORKS

*BL*   *Biographia Literaria,* London (1817) with chapter-numbers;

*CL*   *Collected Letters,* edited by E. L. Griggs, 6 vols. Oxford (1956-) (in progress);

*CN*   *Notebooks,* edited by Kathleen Coburn, 11 vols. New York (1957-) (in progress), with the number of the note;

*CPW*   *Complete Poetical Works,* edited by E. H. Coleridge, 2 vols. Oxford (1912)—for the poems themselves, the page references being largely the same for his one-volume edition of *The Poems* in the Oxford Standard Authors series, Oxford (1912).

## QUOTATIONS

The first complete editions of the notebooks (*CN*) and letters (*CL*) of Coleridge have transformed the subject in recent years, both by furnishing more accurate texts of existing material and by adding much that is new. The editors have naturally chosen to reproduce Coleridge's own vagaries of spelling and punctuation. Now that these texts are on record, however, there seems no good reason for reproducing elsewhere such oddities as are in place in an author's private notes but out of place in a more formal study. My object has been to make sense of Coleridge, and regularizing his text is one way of doing it. For this reason I have modernized his spelling and punctuation, expanded his contractions, ignored his deletions and left his interpolations unspecified. The puzzling details of these texts are now there for anyone to consult, but this has not seemed a proper place in which to record them.

*St John's College, Cambridge*
*September 1965*

# PROLEGOMENA

# CHAPTER ONE

# The Record of Genius

Coleridge's own estimate of his poetic genius seems to have wavered, according to mood, from the highest to the lowest, from exuberance to blank despair. But then the temper of much of his existence was probably mercurial. There is a story told by his daughter how, on his deathbed in July 1834, in the midst of melancholy complaints about the neglect shown him by his relatives, Coleridge suddenly remarked that he was aware of little decay in his faculties, in spite of approaching death, and suddenly added, 'I could even be witty.'[1] The notebooks, which he kept for forty years, leave an equivalent impression of gaiety and gloom in dazzling alternation. At moments he thought himself the worthy collaborator of Wordsworth, whom he always held to be the greatest of all living poets; at others, a facile poetaster who had lost even his facility:

> All my poetic genius (if ever I really possessed any *genius*, and it was not rather a mere general aptitude of talent, and quickness in imitation) is gone, and I have been fool enough to suffer deeply in my mind, regretting the loss, which I attribute to my long and exceedingly severe metaphysical investigations, and these partly to ill-health, and partly to private afflictions . . . (*CL* ii 831).

This is how he wrote to Southey in July 1802, when he was not quite thirty. The passage is one among hundreds that might sadly document his proneness to self-pity; but modern critics have been surprisingly unwilling to consider the contrary evidence for his gaiety and verve, though it is similarly abundant. I continue to find

[1] Letter from Sara Coleridge to her brother Hartley, 5 August 1834; *Coleridge: Studies by Several Hands*, edited by Edmund Blunden and E. L. Griggs, London (1934), p. 227.

this surprising—partly because the mercurial spirit is a matter of common experience, often possessed by literary critics themselves, and readily observable, in any case, among those who lead a literary life; and partly because the works of Coleridge have excited plenty of devoted attention in the twentieth century. There is evidently no lack of readers of Coleridge. But one is left wondering, at times, what they can have been reading, so loud is the chorus of condescension. 'The sad ghost of Coleridge', and 'a handful of golden poems'[2]—these phrases are fully representative of the twentieth-century view. Even Humphry House, in his Clark Lectures of 1951-2, thought it simply obvious that something had gone terribly wrong with Coleridge's career: if it was mistaken to apply the 'carelessly patronising kind' of pity to Coleridge, he argued, this was only because 'a developed, comprehending pity, so far as we are capable of it, a pity like tragic pity, is needed.'[3] T. S. Eliot, in another passage in *The Use of Poetry*, claimed to believe that

> Coleridge was one of those unhappy persons—Donne, I suspect, was such another—of whom one might say that if they had not been poets, they might have made something of their lives, might even have had a career (p. 68).

Here, surely, it must be supposed that Eliot is playing some kind of joke upon his Harvard audience—it is simply not conceivable that an intelligent man can ever have believed this. Still, if such condescension is a joke, it is a joke that has gone far enough, and a good many people have clearly taken it seriously. It is still a great rarity to find a study of Coleridge that does not assume he was a failure, and most modern studies seem to have been written mainly in order to 'explain' his failure. Evidently there is a case for asserting and demonstrating that Coleridge was a great poet, and great not merely in aspiration but by virtue of what he actually did. That is the object of this book. It would be one thing to agree that he was often an unhappy man, his marriage a failure, his health a wreck, and the great love of his life for ever unrequited;

[2] T. S. Eliot, *The Use of Poetry and the Use of Criticism*, London (1933), p. 156; E. K. Chambers, *Coleridge: a Biographical Study*, Oxford (1938), p. 331.
[3] Humphry House, *Coleridge*, London (1953), p. 19.

quite another to suppose that he failed to achieve his promise as a poet and a sage.

To consider, in bare summary, what that achievement was. Hardly a year passed after 1787, when Coleridge turned fifteen, in which he did not write complete poems. His collected poetry, even excluding the verse dramas, amounts to some six hundred pages in the smaller Oxford edition of 1912. His prose works are vast—so vast that they are only now being collected for the first time.[4] They include a mass of political and theological tracts of enormous influence in the nineteenth century, and the *Biographia Literaria* (1817), which has good claim to be considered the most ambitious critical work ever written by an Englishman. This is to ignore the enormous deposits of letters, notes and fragments, some of which are now seeing print for the first time. Paradoxically, and for all their abundance, they have probably contributed to the myth of Coleridge's infertility. And yet they make it clear that at times he would write himself out of an idea in a first draft, lose interest in it and never publish it; the biography of Lessing, for example, which he visited Germany in 1798-9 to write, was fully drafted in some thirty manuscript pages (*CN* 377) before being abandoned for ever. Still, the widespread view that his career was in some sense disappointing must surely have deeper causes than the oddities of his publishing career. It is just because the causes lie so deep in the literary consciousness of the century, in fact, that they are likely to repay investigation.

First, Coleridge as a critic—and as a marketer of his own literary wares—seems to have been strikingly unconcerned with problems of value. This is a genuinely disturbing aspect of his genius, especially in an age in which critical judgments have tended to be put with increasing abruptness and defended or attacked as a matter of life and death. Much literary criticism today, for better or worse, makes a direct moral demand upon the lives and behaviour of those who read it. All this is a world away from the works of Coleridge. His own views of morality could be rigid, even priggish; but he and most of his contemporaries would have been frankly

[4] *The Collected Coleridge*, edited by Kathleen Coburn and others, c. 24 vols. London (1966-).

puzzled by Matthew Arnold's claim that the prime object of literature is to answer the question 'How to live'. And Coleridge's indifference to questions of value can be of direct literary concern.
Whether choosing his own works for publication or describing the
works of another, he seems to care surprisingly little which are
the good poems and which are the bad; and when he does care,
it is not usually to memorable effect. The most theoretical of great
English critics, his criticism is not at its most excellent at those
moments when it is most particular. In his full-dress account of
Wordsworth's poems in the second half of *Biographia Literaria*, for
example, his characterization of the essence of the two Wordsworths
is much more convincing than his choice and discussion of particular poems. His lectures on Shakespeare (1811-12) are more
remarkable for the light they shed upon the art of poetic drama
than for any special revelations they offer concerning this play or
that. And to judge one's own poems, after all, is among the most
exacting of critical tasks. No wonder he was so far from successful
in publishing them in good time to forestall the borrowings of
others or in offering them in such a form as might not strike the
reader, at first glance, as needlessly obscure or outrageously novel.
Some of his surviving poems are admittedly more like chips from
a workshop floor, or at the best works in progress, than self-evident
masterpieces of assured proportions.

For the more patient reader, nonetheless, all this has its own
fascination. Reading the poems of Coleridge is like watching poetry
happen. To read the poems and the prose together is to watch a
single process of trial, error and retrial, and one in which the
poetry as much as the prose is a critical activity. This is in some
ways a self-regarding interest, but it has a lively tradition behind
it. Like most European poets before him, Coleridge took it for
granted that art imitates art as well as the world around itself, and
that what it tells us about may be, as much as anything, the nature
of itself. I do not deny that this is a view of poetry which, however
traditional, demands more patience than every modern reader is
able to bring. It certainly offers no ready certainties, least of all
about the question 'how to live'. It is a view only a professional can
plausibly offer, and one that only those interested in the craftsman-

ship of poetry can readily accept. And, when it speaks of literary 'imitation', it risks confusion with the Aristotelian doctrine of *mimesis*, with which it has nothing whatever to do. 'I do not mean imitation in its largest sense,' as Sir Joshua Reynolds put it in 1774 in his sixth Discourse, addressing students of the Royal Academy, 'but simply the following of the masters, and the advantage to be drawn from the study of their works.'

Perhaps this contrast between Coleridgean delicacy and open-mindedness, on the one hand, and the moral abruptness of much criticism since his day, may be defined more closely by two examples—by his views of Hazlitt and Wordsworth. A note of Coleridge, perhaps written as early as 1799, when Hazlitt was about twenty-one, predicts the parting of the ways between the two men in later life:

> Hazlitt has made the usual mistake of loveless observers—seeing weakness on the surface of a character, he has made no allowance for strength: though seeing characteristic strength (as in Wordsworth), he would be apt enough to make allowance for undiscovered but certainly existing weakness (*CN* 624).

This is a characteristic demand on Coleridge's part to wait and see. The loveless observer sees only half the game, in this view, and then the wrong half. But to see only the other half, as Wordsworth does, is equally an incomplete response:

> Surely always to look at the superficies of objects for the purpose of taking delight in their beauty, and sympathy with their real or imagined life, is as deleterious to the health and manhood of intellect, as always to be peering and unravelling contrivances may be to the simplicity of the affections . . . (*CN* 1,616).

This tentativeness of Coleridge—an aspect of his demand for wholeness of perception—and its accompanying refusal to hurry to a conclusion, are virtues so eccentric in the dogmatic atmosphere of Western literature in the last hundred years that it may have seemed convenient to look for evidence of unfulfilment. Sometimes it is hard to credit that so learned and so gifted a man can have

7

had good reasons for appearing indecisive. Keats, in a letter of December 1817, before he ever met Coleridge, formed from his writings the wildly mistaken notion that his characteristic fault was intellectual impatience: that he 'would let go by a fine isolated verisimilitude caught from the Penetralium of mystery, from being incapable of remaining content with half knowledge'; and he even accused him of an 'irritable reaching after fact and reason'. When he did meet Coleridge, on a walk in Highgate in April 1819, he was in the event amused and impressed by the unending kaleidoscope of his talk ('nightingales, poetry—on poetical sensation—metaphysics—different genera and species of dreams—nightmare . . .') —a juster impression af abundance and verve. In fact he could hardly have made a less accurate charge when he called Coleridge's intelligence 'irritable'. It is gentle and perseverant. His severest rebukes are reserved for those who, like certain reviewers, hurry to a conclusion—for the critic who puts on 'the seven-league boots of self-opinion and strides at once from an illustrator into a Supreme Judge; and blind and deaf fills his three-ounce phial at the water Niagara, and determines positively the greatness of the cataract to be neither more nor less than his three-ounce has been able to receive' (*CN* 3,250). Leigh Hunt, who knew him only slightly, offered in the sixteenth chapter of his *Autobiography* what is perhaps the surest and sanest view of any contemporary: 'a good-natured wizard, very fond of earth . . . A mighty intellect put upon a sensual body'. It is paradoxical that so gentle and so contented a man, as he often was—Hunt, at least, could see clearly enough that the relative inactivity of his later years was ordinary and amiable indolence, and little else—should have been accepted, by so many and for so long, as a poet lost in the wastelands of dogma.

A second source of error has been the abundance of unfinished, even unstarted, projects. It is not only the private notebooks that abound in them—that would be natural enough—but public works like the *Biographia Literaria* as well. Most absurdly of all, even finished works are sometimes offered as if they were unfinished. The case of 'Kubla Khan' is perhaps the strangest of all—a poem that stands high even in English poetry as a work of ordered perfection is offered by the poet himself, nearly twenty years after its composition, as a fragment. Anyone can accept that a writer's head should be full of projects he will never fulfil, and most writers are cautious enough not to set them down; Coleridge, rashly, did set them down, so that his very fertility has survived as evidence of infertility. And sometimes, most paradoxically of all, finished poems like the Dejection Ode are offered as being in themselves instruments of abdication from the vocation of poetry. No European poet before the present century, in all probability, has written as many poems as Coleridge about the difficulty or impossibility of writing a poem. It seems probable that he regarded writing as mental therapy, and it is altogether likely that it was effective in this way: 'The Garden of Boccaccio' is an unusually impressive case, but a case among many in his later years, of how the sheer process of writing a poem could lift the poet, and the poem too, from gloom to joy. Such works present evidence for frustration, it is true; but then simply because they exist, they cannot be taken altogether literally. The 'grief without a pang' from which the Dejection Ode sprang cannot have been utterly 'void, dark and drear', or the Ode could not have happened. A poem is always some sort of an act of faith. And if Coleridge often abdicates as a poet, it is worth remembering that the page is always turned and work—some work or another—always resumed.

Metaphysics, too, has often been thought the ruin of his poetry, and for this rumour Coleridge himself is directly to blame. It is all the more difficult for this reason to contravert it, but the evidence in fact is clear. According to his own account of the matter in the first chapter of the *Biographia Literaria*, metaphysical interests began in his fifteenth year, before he became a poet, and were actively prosecuted in the years 1797-1802, the years of his finest poetic achievement. And these interests were prosecuted not only along with his poetry, but in his poetry too. There is really nothing to be said for the view that philosophy replaced poetry in Coleridge's career. It is a view that takes secret comfort, perhaps, from an inner conviction that poetry has no business to be more than faintly philosophical, that there is even some inherent reason why a man cannot be a poet and a philosopher too. But this is surely a matter in which judgment should be suspended: a philosophical poem is credible if and when it is there. 'Why so violent against meta-physics in poetry?' is a question Coleridge once fired at a friend in a letter of May 1796 (*CL* i 215), and the challenge remains an arresting one. Philosophical interests cannot be thought to have killed or impaired Coleridge's genius as a poet: they began before his highest achievements in poetry and continued hand in hand with them; and much of the late verse, as I hope to show, is too good to be dismissed on any score. Coleridge's own view of what philo-sophy could do is certainly open to the objection of being vague and over-ambitious, but it is perfectly consistent with his life as a poet. 'What is it,' he wrote in optimistic vein in October 1803, 'that I employ my metaphysics on?', and his answer was:

> To expose the folly and the legerdemain of those who have thus abused the blessed organ of language; to support all old and vener-able truths; to support, to kindle, to project, to make the reason spread light over our feelings, to make our feelings diffuse vital warmth through our reason (*CN* 1,623).

This offers the outline of an account of what a philosophical poetry might be like. It also has a good deal of the impulsiveness, the buttonholing urgency, and the eager earnestness, that are at least as characteristic of Coleridge as self-pity. Indeed it raises the sus-picion, like much else in Coleridge, that the character of the Ancient Mariner had something of facetious self-portraiture in it, and per-haps it had. Dr Gillman, his first biographer, drew the analogy, and it may have been Coleridge's own.[5]

The rich temptations of scholarship, too, have sometimes proved the undoing of Coleridge's reputation. It is not easy to talk of the great ancestor-study of Coleridge's intellectual background, John Livingston Lowes's *The Road to Xanadu* (1927), or of its many successors, without a sense of gratitude. But there is clear sense in which these studies have led away from the poems. Of course the temptation is easily felt. Coleridge's reading was so vast and

---

[5] James Gillman, *The Life of Coleridge*, London (1838): 'He delighted many of the strangers he met in his saunterings through the cloisters [of Christ's Hospital], arrested and riveted the attention of the passer-by whom, like his 'Ancient Mariner', he held by a spell' (p. 36).

so seductive that the urge to use his poems as pass-keys into such worlds as seventeenth-century mysticism or eighteenth-century travel-books is an almost enviable aberration. Certainly Lowes's study of the sources—at times the unconscious sources—of 'The Ancient Mariner' and 'Kubla Khan' in Coleridge's half-remembered reading will stand as a permanent monument to historical criticism. But it is one thing to ask how a poem may have emerged from the stored memory of the poet, another to ask what it is—however much the answer to the one question may help in answering the other. And the formal interest is not an eccentric one. To study the formality of Coleridge's poems, which is my object here, is a natural undertaking enough in view of his own aspirations towards the 'esemplastic' and the shapely. All his life he was fascinated by problems of metre (*CN* 372-3, 1,848). In his doctrine of poetic creation the imagination was above all a 'shaping spirit', and poetry 'a rationalized dream' (*CN* 2,086), a thing ordered as well as felt. Even as a schoolboy at Christ's Hospital in the 1780's he had learned from the best of his teachers that poetry, 'even that of the loftiest and, seemingly, that of the wildest odes, had a logic of its own as severe as that of science; and more difficult, because more subtle, and dependent on more, and more fugitive, causes' (*BL* i). The 'logic' of a Coleridgean poem is what I should like more nearly to approach. But one last misapprehension still stands in the way.

There seems to have been an abiding suspicion on the part of literary historians over the past hundred years that aspiration rather than solid achievement was the true virtue of the English Romantics. The prejudice was established momentously in Matthew Arnold's second series of *Essays in Criticism* (1888), where the Romantics emerge in memorable caricature as amiably provincial clowns, with many of the gifts of the heart and few of the head: blundering, aimless, gifted but improvident of their gifts. Wordsworth, whom he held to have had no style, simply let Nature 'take the pen out of his hand, and . . . write for him with her own bare, sheer, penetrating power.' Keats, though 'a great spirit', had in him 'something underbred and ignoble, as of a youth ill brought up', and as a poet could be allowed little more than 'natural magic'. Shelley, though a high-minded gentleman, talked nonsense about tyrants

11

and priests and wrote poetry that was 'not entirely sane'. Arnold's judgments, with many variations of emphasis, are still influential. And in their wake has followed the still more damaging judgment that the fragmentary was, in romantic terms, an end in itself. Not only did the Romantics fail to compose fully matured works: according to a later view, they did not even seek to do so. The notion finds its best support in the *Fragmente* (1798) of Friedrich Schlegel and in Novalis's theory and practice of poetry, both of which contain clear enough statements of such a doctrine.[6] But it would nonetheless be rash to attribute the doctrine of the Germans to their English contemporaries. There is conclusive evidence, after all, that Coleridge meant to finish 'Christabel', Wordsworth *The Recluse*, and Keats *Hyperion*, and no reason to doubt that Byron's completion of *Don Juan* was frustrated only by death. And the critical views of the romantic poets in England cannot be reconciled with a love of the fragmentary for its own sake. It is true that many views of the age on the subject of artistic unity, including Coleridge's, were deliberately paradoxical on this issue. Blake in 1820 held that 'every poem must necessarily be a perfect unity'; but he added that 'when a work has unity, it is as much in a part as in the whole: the torso is as much a unity as the Laocoon'. And yet there seems no good reason to deny to a statement like this its face-value: that the total structure of a finished work may be deduced from its part. Blake had made a similar point in his annotations (*c.* 1808) to Reynolds's *Discourses*, when he preferred the prints of Raphael and Michelangelo to finished paintings of Rubens: 'These things that you call finished are not even begun; how can they then be finished? The man who does not know the beginning never can know the end of art.'[7] The tendency to see everything new after 1800 is so strong that it is easy to forget that Blake's paradox is a familiar neoclassical one, however novel the purposes to which he may have wished to put it. Reynolds himself, who was Blake's aversion, held in his twelfth Discourse that even fragments are excellent if by a master; and David Hume, who in his literary

---

[6] Cf. Edgar Wind, *Art and Anarchy*, London (1963), pp. 42f., 140f.
[7] William Blake, *Complete Writings*, edited by Geoffrey Keynes, London (1957), pp. 778, 449.

judgments seems the very archetype of the neoclassic, in his essay 'Of Tragedy' quoted with approval a familiar saying of the Elder Pliny concerning the special excellence of works left unfinished by a great artist at his death: 'the broken lineaments of the piece, and the half-formed idea of the painter, are carefully studied; and our very grief for that curious hand, which had been stopped by death, is an additional encrease to our pleasure'. No one would think of deducing from this that Hume or Reynolds thought fragments better than the whole works, and I believe that what Blake and Coleridge are saying, so far as it can be confined to this single issue, can most naturally be interpreted in a similar way. Certainly the evidence needs to be pushed hard to yield a doctrine of the fragmentary. The subtitle 'A Fragment', which Coleridge added to 'Kubla Khan' when he came to publish it in 1816, reads more naturally as an apology than as a boast, especially as the preface that follows immediately upon it is apologetic in a high degree ('published . . . rather as a psychological curiosity than on the ground of any supposed poetic merits'). Leigh Hunt, collecting his own poems for the edition of 1832, considered the publication of fragments suicidal for a poet's reputation: 'Random thoughts and fillings-up are a poet's *felo de se*' (p. xiii). There seems no good reason to doubt that the romantic poets believed as much in whole and finished works as any previous generation of English poets. That they found them, at times, more difficult to achieve is another matter.

But then the Arnoldian view of the English Romantics as pathetic provincials, outside the main current of European civilization and provincially contemptuous of the lasting virtues of classic form, represents a very precise inversion of the truth. This is the ultimate condescension, and one that must seem oddest of all to a continental historian of literature, who commonly accepts what most nineteenth-century Europeans accepted: that England was the natural leader of the intellectual movement that came to be called Romanticism, and that in Wordsworth, Scott and Byron, most notably, it offered literary stimulants with which France and Germany could not claim to compete. Arnold's affectation of cosmopolitan wisdom is the less convincing when one reflects how badly out of step is his view of the English Romantics with the Anglophilia of Goethe or Hugo or Pushkin. At times he seems uncomfortably aware of the point himself: in his essay on Byron (1881), for example, he quotes Goethe's magnificent compliment to Byron as 'the greatest talent of the century', but only in order to qualify and depreciate it. The point may perhaps be pushed further home. A distortion of our critical language has tended to disguise the fact that the English Romantics were pre-eminent in those virtues commonly attributed to classicism: that they were *more* successful than eighteenth-century poets in composing achieved poems in the given literary kinds. My chief purpose here will be to substantiate this claim in relation to one romantic poet—to show that Coleridge wrote, and knowingly wrote, poems which belong to the established forms. This is not a claim that could be made for the dominant poetic figures of the preceding century. Dryden, Pope and Cowper are not poets whose reputations are in any danger, and it is no great detraction to argue that a similar claim could not be made for them; it would be implausible to suggest, for example, that Dryden's *Absalom and Achitophel* or Pope's *Essay on Man*, taken as a whole, belong to clearly established literary kinds of which they are complete examples. This was a truth broadly recognized in the eighteenth century itself. The failure of that age to fulfil its prime literary ambition and to re-create the greatest of all the poetic forms, as it was held to be—that of the epic—was widely accepted and bemoaned by the Augustan poets and critics themselves. Johnson makes it very clear, in his lives of Dryden and Pope, that in his view their achievement was stylistic rather than structural: they remade English verse, 'improved our numbers'—but *Absalom and Achitophel* is brilliantly ramshackle, the *Essay on Man* seductively vapid. The picture Johnson offers in the *Lives* is still a convincing one: that of a poetry of incidental brilliance, of high excellence subsisting only in the parts. Even *The Rape of the Lock*, where the structural problem is exquisitely solved, is hardly an example of a solution of a classical kind: the 'preternatural agents' of sylphs and gnomes, Johnson agrees, are 'happily adapted to the purposes of the poem', but they are in themselves an admission that by the eighteenth century the classical machinery of the epic and of the

14

mock-epic could not be made to work: 'The heathen deities can no longer gain attention: we should have turned away from a contest between Venus and Diana.' Later ages have found the Augustan age classical in its achievement: the Augustans themselves, more often than not, saw classic form as an aspiration rather than a fact.

To contrast this with such romantic achievements as Blake's *Songs of Innocence and Experience*, Coleridge's 'Ancient Mariner', Wordsworth's Immortality Ode, Byron's *Don Juan*, Shelley's *Prometheus Unbound*, or the Odes of Keats is to enter another world. The virtues of these poems are not incidental but innate. They succeed not in their occasional merits, but by the sheer weight of what they are. Formality and purpose, in these cases, are self-evidently at one. The Immortality Ode is not only a statement of Wordsworth's doctrine of Nature: it is a successful ode in an ancestral line that leads back to the Pindaric Odes of Cowley, and there are good reasons why it should choose (and at times defy) the formality of this established literary kind. 'The Ancient Mariner' succeeds *as a ballad*, intricate as may be the reasons for its formal success. Byron's imitation of the Italian comic epic justifies itself more simply: the thing he is attempting, in its pertness and irreverence, is genuinely like what Pulci and other Italians had done; and where the nature of the two languages makes it differ, as it notably does in the matter of rhyme, Byron makes a comic virtue of this difference too. This is the bluntest of outlines of the formal achievements of the English Romantics—an achievement, it must be confessed, not so much under-estimated as simply unnoticed—but the issue of romantic formality needs at the outset to be put in blunt terms. As it is, the heritage of Arnold has proved a succession of misunderstandings. His condescension towards the intellectual weapons of the romantic poets has been succeeded in this century by the outright contempt of judges as influential as Irving Babbitt, T. S. Eliot and Professor Yvor Winters. And even the inevitable revival of interest in romanticism, in the shape it has taken, has tended silently to accept the premises upon which the anti-romantic case was based. Professor Northrop Frye and his followers have more recently made plausible, and at times weighty, defences of the intellectual and mythological equipment of the romantic poets. But one is often left with the suspicion that what they say could, more often than not, be as well said of bad poems as of good ones. The myth-hunters have been helpful in exegesis, and certainly Arnold's lofty attacks upon the alleged provincialism of the English Romantics can best be rebutted by appeals to the wealth of their intellectual sources and to the plain fact of their acknowledged leadership of nineteenth-century Europe. It matters even more to insist that they wrote good poems, and that the excellence of these poems, though distinct and of its time, is verifiable by the poetic standards of any age.

# CHAPTER TWO

# The Imitative Art

The logic of a poem is a fact of its formal design. But Coleridge's poems strikingly lack a single design. Unlike Wordsworth's, they impress above all by the diversity of the models they employ: in fact they might almost serve as an encyclopaedia of English poetic forms before the age of Victoria. In their age, it is true, this diversity was exceptional only as a matter of degree; the commonest kind of collection of English poetry in the 1770's and 1780's, when Coleridge was a boy, was the miscellany, or assemblage of 'specimens'—usually translations and imitations from Greek, Latin and Italian, and perhaps from some more exotic language such as Persian or Old Norse as well. The characteristic poetic exercise of the age was already pastiche. And the twentieth century has on the whole proved more hospitable to this kind of activity in practice than in theory. In Ezra Pound and T. S. Eliot, for example, it can offer two of the greatest *pasticheurs* in the history of the language—and yet one of Eliot's admirers in the 1930's thought it necessary to rescue his hero from the charge as if from some damaging imputation: '. . . the relation of *Gerontion* to Middleton and his contemporaries must not be allowed to suggest that Mr Eliot's verse has anything in it of pastiche'.[1] But the failure has been a purely critical one, and the age has continued to excel in the very property which it condemns. It is simply that the notion of poetry as a great 'grocery shop' of language, as Friedrich Schlegel once called German poetry in his own day—as a place in which the linguistic products of many places and many ages are stored ready for use —has fallen out of literary currency. Ruskin, who in early middle age seems never to have heard of *Biographia Literaria* ('I have

[1] F. R. Leavis, *New Bearings in English Poetry*, London (1932), p. 82.

never heard of the Coleridge and Wordsworth dispute—where can I find an account of it?'), made the elementary mistake of thinking that the 'Ancient Mariner' was in everyday English: 'What can possibly be simpler than every word of the 'Ancient Mariner'? . . . It is absolute pure—common English'; and in the same letter of December 1843 he shows how the demand for moral rigour in literature was already beginning to block all other interests—'Christabel' was 'a mere rhapsody', so far as he could see: 'There is no moral truth, no system or meaning in it from beginning to end'.[2] Ezra Pound, too, has tended to use the term 'pastiche' as a term of profound contempt.[3] Parody, perhaps, is the only form of literary imitation now commonly allowed to have a distinct existence, and that an inferior one. It is probably significant that English does not at present possess terms in which to describe what Coleridge is doing to the medieval ballad in 'The Ancient Mariner', or Keats to *Paradise Lost* in *Hyperion*. 'Parody' is a comic term, after all, and 'The Ancient Mariner' and *Hyperion* are not comic poems, though the interest taken in the ingenuity of a pun or witticism is not utterly foreign to the interest they have to offer; it is 'a source of the magical power of "The Ancient Mariner",' it has already been noticed, 'that the inside can be felt to be far from the outside . . . and yet somehow they keep fitting one another perfectly.'[4] 'Travesty' is a word which, if only it had maintained its original sense (to put on the clothing, the literary dress, of another), might have perfectly filled my present need; but since its first recorded use in English, in Samuel Butler's *Hudibras* (1674) (I iii n. 196), it has always suggested the grotesque and the debased. 'Pastiche' is a word I have used already, and must use again, but it evidently lacks the dignity, or even the neutrality, that the case demands: what is needed is a term severe enough to be used in

[2] *Complete Works of Ruskin*, edited by E. T. Cook and Alexander Wedderburn, London (1903-12), vol. iv, pp. 391-2. His chapter in *Modern Painters* entitled 'Of Ideas of Imitation' (vol. iii, pp. 99-103) suggests that for Ruskin artistic 'imitation' could only mean the imitation of natural objects, a contemptible art akin to mere sleight-of-hand.

[3] Ezra Pound, *Literary Essays*, edited by T. S. Eliot, London (1954), p. 216 (from an essay of 1914).

[4] William Empson, 'The Ancient Mariner', *Critical Quarterly*, vi (1964), p. 319.

such a context as '*Hyperion* is a pastiche of *Paradise Lost*'. The word I shall commonly use, then, will be 'imitation', striving back towards a usage familiar enough in classical Latin and in the Renaissance, and recently revived by Mr Robert Lowell in his *Imitations* of 1962. Roger Ascham in the second book of his *Schole-master* (1570), offers a lively English account, drawn partly from Cicero, Quintilian and Erasmus, of what he calls 'a facultie to expresse livelie and perfitelie that example which ye go about to follow'; and Abraham Cowley in his preface to the Odes of 1656 employed the word, for the first time in the records of the language, to describe a kind of poem. Perhaps Dryden offers the best guide of all; in describing the art of poetic translation in the preface to his version of *Ovid's Epistles* (1680), he proffered this late but influential definition:

> The third way [of translation, after metaphrase and paraphrase] is that of imitation, where the translator (if now he has not lost that name) assumes the liberty not only to vary from the words and sense, but to forsake them both as he sees occasion; and taking only some general hints from the original, to run division on the ground-work [i.e. to invent variations, as if on a musical theme], as he pleases. Such is Mr Cowley's practice in turning two Odes of Pindar, and one of Horace, into English.

Three-quarters of a century later, Johnson adopted this somewhat too strict view of the word in his *Dictionary* (1755):

> A method of translating looser than paraphrase, in which modern examples and illustrations are used for ancient, or domestick for foreign.

Both these definitions are good places to start, but not to stop; and Johnson should have seen, as he seems to have done already in his 121st *Rambler* (14 May 1751), where he complains about the current vogue of Spenserian imitations, that an imitation need not be a translation at all: 'the style of Spenser might by long labour be justly copied,' Johnson concluded, 'but life is surely given us for higher purposes . . .' An imitation may be a representation of a total style, in fact, as Keats tried to represent Milton's; or of a total work, but without line by-line correspondence, as Pope imitated Horace. Dryden came close to anticipating the point in 1680—'the translator (if now he has not lost that name)'—but I shall have to use this licence much more vigorously than he. Johnson, by the time he came to write the *Life of Pope*, evidently understood that the 'mode of imitation' was a kind of poetry rather than a kind of translation, 'in which the ancients are familiarised by adapting their sentiments to modern topicks, by making Horace say of Shakespeare what he originally said of Ennius, and accommodating his satires on Pantolabus and Nomentanus to the flatterers and prodigals of our own time.' He went on to suggest, without much investigation, that the English pioneers were Oldham and Rochester in the 1670's and 1680's—'at least I remember no instances more ancient.' It is now known that Oldham and Rochester had English predecessors before the Restoration in Denham and Cowley;[5] but at all events, the mid-seventeeth century is clearly the poetic moment in which this form arises in England, and Roman satire is the form it commonly chooses to imitate. It dominates a large part of eighteenth-century English poetry, still mainly in the way of satire; and spreads outwards into exotic forms in the nineteenth century, a matter which forms the subject of this book. One decisive difference emerges at once between the seventeenth- and the eighteenth-century practice of imitation: the seventeenth century, with the striking exception of Rochester, who in the 'Allusion to Horace' of 1675 predicts the achievement of Pope and Johnson, usually offered its imitations as substitutes for the originals—evidently for those who did not know the classical languages, or did not know them well. A seventeenth-century imitation is commonly, as Dryden had said, a kind of translation. Pope's imitations of Horace in the 1730's, and Johnson's of Juvenal soon after, are by contrast 'allusions', in which the reader is asked to take pleasure in what Johnson in the *Life of Pope* called the 'unexpected parallels': 'the comparison requires

[5] Harold F. Brooks, 'The "Imitation" in English Poetry before Pope', *Review of English Studies*, xxv (1949); cf. Richard McKeon, 'The Concept of Imitation in Antiquity' in *Critics and Criticism*, ed. R. S. Crane, Chicago (1952), pp. 168-74; Mary Lascelles, 'Johnson and Juvenal', in *New Light on Dr Johnson*, ed. F. W. Hilles, New Haven (1959); E. C. Riley, *Cervantes's Theory of the Novel*, Oxford (1962), pp. 61f.

knowledge of the original, which will likewise often detect strained applications'. Such imitation triumphs by unexpected felicity, adds Johnson, where 'the thoughts are unexpectedly applicable, and the parallels lucky.'

It is best to admit at the start that contemporary man is cut off from this world of experience, so that the present chapter, digressive as it may at first appear, is a matter of plain necessity. However we may judge the success of the school of Pound, classical imitation, at any rate, is not a live poetic form of the first significance. And what cuts us off from this world of poetry is above all a vast educational revolution. Any Renaissance schoolboy must have known what poetic imitation was like, regardless of what he called it, and Dryden in 1680 was only codifying a set of practices he had learned at Westminster School in the 1640's. In an introductory note to his version of the third satire of Persius (1693), near the end of his life, he recalled after a lapse of half a century how he had prepared the same task as a schoolboy 'for a Thursday night's exercise; and [I] believe that it, and many other of my exercises of this nature in English verse, are still in the hands of my learned master, the Reverend Doctor Busby'. The custom of encouraging boys to write English imitations of classical poems may have been more advanced at Westminster, the great nurse of English poets in the sixteenth and seventeenth centuries, than in other schools. There is a surviving account of the daily routine early in the seventeenth century, which shows that every afternoon the boys

> repeated a leafe or two out of some booke of rhetoricall figures or choice proverbs and sentences collected by the M[aste]r for that use. After that, they were practised in translating some dictamina out of Lat. or Gr., and sometimes turning Lat. and Gr. verse into English verse.[6]

But the writing of imitations in one language or another had been practised in schools throughout Europe for a century and more before Dryden was born, and survives, vestigially, in some schools

---

[6] G. F. Russell Barker, *Memoir of Richard Busby*, London (1895), p. 50, from an anonymous manuscript in the Public Record Office said to be in Archbishop Laud's hand.

to this day. Johnson, in his *Life of Milton*, writes as if English imitations were a commonplace exercise in eighteenth-century schools; Milton's metrical versions of two psalms, he writes, executed at the age of fifteen, 'would in any numerous school have obtained praise, but not excited wonder'. Lists of word-collocations such as the *Index rhetoricus*, and later the *Gradus*, were used to help boys to compose in the classical manner, the task being to catch the essence and spirit of a great original. According to Charles Hoole (1610-1667), a Yorkshire schoolmaster who wrote a handbook for Restoration teachers,

> the Master indeed should cause his scholars to recite a piece of Ovid or Virgil in his hearing now and then, that the very tune of these pleasant verses may be imprinted in their mindes, so that when ever they are put to compose a verse, they make it glide as even as those in their authours.[7]

This refers to the writing of Latin verses; but Dryden tells us he was taught to imitate in English too, and it is not surprising if most English poets before this century began their careers by writing imitations, in the broadest sense of the term, of Greek and Latin poets. Marlowe began with a version of Lucan, and followed it with the highly Ovidian *Hero and Leander* and the intensely Virgilian *Dido*; Shakespeare, in *Venus and Adonis*, with an imitation of Ovid; Spenser and Pope with Virgilian pastorals; Cowley and Dryden with 'Pindaric' odes; Johnson and Byron with Juvenalic satires. The tradition had its frivolous side: over 120 parodies and imitations of Gray's *Elegy* (1751) are known to have been published by 1800. Imitation, in the sixteenth, seventeenth and eighteenth centuries, and even after, was the mode by which poets, calling on their familiar schoolboy experience in the classical languages, taught themselves to be English poets. Coleridge, who in the first chapter of the *Biographia Literaria* took a balanced and middle-aged view of the matter, thought some aspects of the tradition harmful. Imitation seemed to him to account for some of the worst and shabbiest devices of Augustan poetry—the sense he

[7] *A New Discovery of the Old Art of Teaching Schoole*, London (1660), p. 188; cf. M. L. Clarke, *Classical Education in Britain*, *1500-1900*, Cambridge (1959), pp. 38-40.

had, even in the exercise of Pope's 'matchless talent and ingenuity', that the outcome was not so much poetry as 'thoughts *translated* into the language of poetry'. Reviewing his early education, he felt that the ancient tradition of teaching Latin was largely to blame:

> This style of poetry, which I have characterized above as translations of prose thoughts into poetic language, had been kept up by, if it did not wholly arise from, the custom of writing Latin verses, and the great importance attached to these exercises in our public schools . . . A youth . . . must first prepare his thoughts, and then pick out from Virgil, Horace, Ovid, or perhaps more compendiously, from his *Gradus*, halves and quarters of lines in which to embody them.

But then Coleridge's mature contempt for the *Gradus* is based on his earliest experience as a poet: his first surviving poems, written in his mid-teens, are English imitations of Horace and Anacreon, along with an animated schoolboy parody of Pindar, 'A Mathematical Problem'. Comic parody and reverent imitation, especially of Horatian models, go hand in hand in these schoolboy exercises. And yet they are the merest starting-point. His later achievement as a poet was to stretch the principle of imitation so far beyond these familiar classical models—beyond even the worlds of English medieval and Renaissance poetry—as to enrich it beyond all expectation. Words, as he came to see, possess what linguists now call an 'associative field'; they entice the poet and endanger him too, in an historically conscious age, with the wealth of their past literary associations—associations of a complexity that no Gradus could encompass. And yet poems are written in words and in nothing else. This has proved the inviting dilemma of every English poet since romanticism: to borrow, to pervert, even to abuse, the languages other poets have made, and yet to create out of them works which float free of their past and enter into a separate existence. The poet may be as original as you please, 'but still the heart doth need a language', as Coleridge put it in his version of Schiller's *Wallenstein* (1800): the most original poet is an inheritor too. In this difficult and fundamental sense his poetry, from the start, was always an outcome of his critical genius.

My purpose in this chapter is to show how, in its theory and practice of imitation, the new poetry of the Regency was distinct from that of the Augustans and of the Renaissance, and yet not discontinuous from it; and to show how suggestive, in a more limited degree, romantic theories of the subject were. I have no wish to offer Coleridge's poems as oddities in their time. On the contrary, they are 'romantic' precisely in the awareness they suggest of the variety of literary experience in the European tradition. True, it has long been a commonplace to say that the Romantics were interested in the past; but thoughts are meant to fly, in such discussions, to the tushery of the lesser Waverley novels—those on the Crusades or the age of Elizabeth I—while forgetting the intelligent erudition and the grasp of social history of such novels as *Waverley* and *Old Mortality*. We think of the absurdities of the Gothic Revival in England, and forget that it was among the first intelligent comments in all Europe on the glories of medieval architecture. Our pleasure in the orientalism of the Brighton Pavilion cannot now be altogether unpatronizing; but when Nash built it in 1787 for the Prince of Wales, later George IV, it represented an astounding insight into a civilization remote in space as well as in time. A glance at two literary events, one in 1812, the other in 1819, which stirred their own age and which are now easily overlooked, may bring the period into sharper focus.

In 1812 James and Horace Smith, the sons of a London solicitor, published a collection of twenty-one verse parodies under the title *Rejected Addresses*, to appear on the very day that Drury Lane Theatre re-opened. Its success was enormous: it was promptly welcomed by Jeffrey in the *Edinburgh Review* and passed through eighteen editions in twenty years. It seems to have been especially appreciated by the very poets it parodied, and the temper of the age can best be indicated by the story that one eminent versifier, Thomas Campbell, objected to his own exclusion. Coleridge was not consistently tolerant on the subject of parody, as his surprisingly resentful reaction to Peter Bayley's mediocre imitations of *Lyrical Ballads* in his *Poems* of 1803 suggests (*CN* 1,673); but in a long footnote to the first chapter of the *Biographia* he was later to make fun of anyone who supposed parody to be a hurtful insult by recounting the story of an amateur poet who had sought an introduction to him, hesitating only on the grounds that he had written a parody of his 'Ancient Mariner':

> I assured my friend that if the epigram was a good one, it would only increase my desire to become acquainted with the author, and begg'd to hear it recited: when, to my no less surprise than amusement, it proved to be one which I had myself some time before written and inserted in the *Morning Post*:

To the Author of the 'Ancient Mariner':

> Your poem must eternal be,
> Dear sir! it cannot fail,
> For 'tis incomprehensible
> And without head or tail.

Jeffrey's review of *Rejected Addresses*, which confirmed the success of the volume, establishes certain facts at once: that 'imitation' was the term still used in Regency criticism, as it had been since before Dryden, to describe the wide range of forms stretching from parody to a kind of loose translation; and that it was an activity that unites Augustan and romantic poetry, however much the range of models to be imitated may divide the one from the other. Jeffrey, after all, is a critic close enough to the Augustan tradition to count here, and he quotes Burke's parody of Bolingbroke, *A Vindication of Natural Society* (1756), as 'the most perfect specimen' of imitation in English. His review even helps to show how in that age words worked to describe the various kinds. The *Rejected Addresses*, says Jeffrey, are 'a series of imitations of the style and manner of the most celebrated living writers', though he later tightens the argument by speaking of them as possessing 'the features both of burlesque and of imitation', as if recalling the serious purposes to which Dryden and Johnson had put the latter term. His phrase 'a mere parody or travesty' adds to 'burlesque' a second and a third term, all fully in play in English for a century and more before Jeffrey, to describe satiric imitation, and he goes on to offer a prescription for literary caricature:

> the resemblance [between parody and its original] . . . can only
> be rendered striking by exaggerating a little . . . all that is peculiar
> and characteristic in the model; . . . just as the course of a river, or
> a range of mountains, is more distinctly understood when laid down
> on a map or plan, than when studied in their natural proportions.[8]

Seven years after the astounding success of the *Rejected Addresses*,
a little skirmish of parodies was conducted by the second generation
of Romantics against the first. On hearing that the middle-aged
Wordsworth was about to publish his youthful poem *Peter Bell*,
John Hamilton Reynolds, a friend of Keats, who knew the poem
only by hearsay, rushed into print in April 1819 with his own
parody of the poem, which was reviewed by Keats in the *Examiner*
—the 'ante-natal Peter', as Shelley gleefully called it, as it antici-
pated the poem it parodied by several days, and successfully
imitated Wordsworth's five-line stanza and the Wordsworthian
flatness of tone. Reynolds may have been the author of a second
parody, *Benjamin the Waggoner*, and he probably wrote the third
parody of August 1819, *The Dead Asses: a Lyrical Ballad*, which
is shorter and better pointed than *Benjamin*.[9] And in October, at
Florence, Shelley wrote yet another parody, *Peter Bell the Third*,
stimulated by a reading of the *Examiner* reviews and, as Shelley
boasted in the dedication, 'considerably the dullest of the three'.

These two literary incidents are retold here as evidences of that
large and neglected aspect of the romantic intelligence that devoted
itself deliberately to the imitative art—an aspect obvious enough
to its own age, and flowering in the 1820's and 1830's in the comic
genius of Hood, and yet one from which Victorian and modern
critics have tended on the whole to avert their eyes. Such poems as
openly represent the romantic fascination with literary styles are
usually hustled in modern editions into sections entitled 'Juvenilia'
or 'Translations', with odd results. Not many people, probably,
now know that Shelley translated some considerable parts of Homer,
Virgil, and Dante, as well as scenes from Goethe's *Faust*; or that
Coleridge translated Schiller's *Wallenstein*; or that Keats wrote

[8] *Edinburgh Review*, xx (1812), pp. 436, 437.
[9] Cf. G. L. Marsh, 'The *Peter Bell* Parodies of 1819', *Modern Philology* xl (1943),
who prints excerpts from *The Dead Asses*.

one entire Shakespearean tragedy, and started another; or that Byron translated, with predictable brilliance, the first canto of the fifteenth-century Italian comic epic which underlies the triumph of his late style, the *Morgante Maggiore* of Pulci. The poem in which Keats's genius first asserts itself undeniably, the 1816 sonnet 'On First Looking into Chapman's Homer', is fittingly the celebration of a literary debt which might stand as a motto to this aspect of the romantic achievement:

> Much have I travell'd in the realms of gold,
> And many goodly states and kingdoms seen;
> Round many western islands have I been
> Which bards in fealty to Apollo hold.

That the isles are 'western' only is a generous admission, on the part of the poet, that he is Greekless; but the sonnet as a whole asserts his right to make free of the Elizabethan Chapman and of the Greeks as well. The career of Shelley illustrates the same principle in its most extravagant form: no English poet in any age, surely, has ever imitated with such continuous temerity. Keats's career moves briefly, and with relative caution, from an early passion for Spenser—his earliest poem is entitled 'Imitation of Spenser'—to a passion for Shakespeare, whose portrait stood over his desk during the great year (1818-19) in which he achieved everything; and that year included an unfinished imitation of Milton in *Hyperion* and the rediscovery of the neoclassical ode in the spring of 1819. But with Shelley there is no limit to ambition, and scarcely any end to the catalogue of the imitated: Aeschylus, Dante, Shakespeare, Goethe . . . There is something at times inadequate, it must also be confessed, in the failure of Shelley's inspirational theories of poetic creation to take measure of what he is doing. The preface to *The Revolt of Islam*, a narrative poem in Spenserian stanzas, proclaims that

> I am unwilling to tread in the footsteps of any who have preceded me. I have sought to avoid the imitation of any style of language or versification peculiar to the original minds of which it is the character . . .

27

though he later offers a clear reason for preferring Spenserian stanzas to blank verse. The fact is that Shelley is not only the boldest of English romantic imitators, but also at times the least conscious. There are moments when he hardly knows what he does, or even seems to want to know. The *Cenci* was a deliberate Shakespearean imitation, it is true, and not the only case of deliberation; but often his best poetry seems, in its choice of sources or echoes, unwilled and spontaneous; and the vast storehouse of an erudite mind gives up its riches in a manner so unpredictable, so far beneath the surface of rational choices, as often to seem beyond the reach of deliberation and of art.

Byron is an opposite case: Byron, who believed in an Augustan continuity, was bound to feel consciously that imitation was the only road. He set out to be Pope, and imitated, in his earliest poems, such ancestors as Catullus, Horace, and Juvenal—the very sources of the Augustan spring. The first step, in his view, was to choose the right models to imitate: the Augustans, not the primitive Eliza-bethans and Jacobeans admired by Lamb, Shelley and Keats. If Pope is the 'touch-stone' of taste, as he called him in a letter of September 1821, then it is

> a great error to suppose the present a high age of English poetry —it is equivalent to the age of Statius or Silius Italicus, except that instead of imitating the Virgils of our language, they are 'trying back' (to use a hunting phrase) upon the Ennius's and Lucilius's who had better have remained in their obscurity.[10]

The role of imitation in the poetry of the English Romantics, as in the poetry of their predecessors, is clearly an enormous one; and it would be tempting to apply the same kind of analysis to the novel of the Regency: to Jane Austen's early literary parodies in her juvenilia, and to her comment on the Gothic novel in *Northanger Abbey* (1818); or to Peacock's re-handling of the literary dialogue in *Headlong Hall* (1816) and after. Much romantic criticism, un-fortunately, tends to lead away from the truth: there is a 'romantic' view of the English Romantics as vital barbarians who shattered an age of manners and of mannerisms, a view which the Romantics

[10] *Byron: a Self-Portrait*, edited by Peter Quennell, vol. ii, London (1950), p. 666.

themselves were sometimes happy enough to adopt. Wordsworth's Advertisement to the first edition of *Lyrical Ballads* (1798) admits that the 'Ancient Mariner' was 'professedly written in imitation of the *style*, as well as of the spirit of the elder poets'; but he writes as if only Percy's *Reliques* stood behind these poems, and then only behind the contribution of Coleridge, and as if his own poems were simply 'a natural delineation of human passions'. Hazlitt puts this mythical view of English romantic poetry very accurately in his discussion of Wordsworth twenty years later, in his *Lectures on the English Poets* (1818): 'All was to be natural and new. Nothing that was established was to be tolerated.' Most people, to this day, are probably quite unaware that Wordsworth had literary precedents like Hannah More's *Cheap Repository Tracts* of 1795-8, or the numerous literary ballads published in late eighteenth-century reviews, when he adapted the broadsheet ballad to a moral purpose: it disturbs the abiding image of a poet whose study was in the fields. John Clare openly demanded that his poems should be regarded as outside literature, in the familiar sense of the word:

> I found the poems in the fields,
> And only wrote them down ('Sighing for Retirement').

But Blake put the sensible and traditional case with heavy emphasis and a new edge: 'Imitation *is* criticism,' he wrote in his copy of Reynolds; and 'the difference between a bad artist and a good one is: the bad artist seems to copy a great deal; the good one really does copy a great deal.'[11] Hazlitt too, in his eternal quest for the fine phrase, hit upon something like the truth of the matter —that the romantic achievement is a literary achievement like the Augustan, and unlike it only in the range of its models; but then, still questing for phrases, he glanced away into absurdity. His chapter on Coleridge in *The Spirit of the Age* (1825) opens:

> The present is an age of talkers, and not of doers; and the reason is, that the world is growing old. We are so far advanced in the Arts and Sciences, that we live in retrospect, and doat on past

[11] *The Complete Writings of William Blake*, edited by Geoffrey Keynes, London (1957), pp. 453, 456.

achievements. The accumulation of knowledge has been so great, that we are lost in wonder at the height it has reached . . . Mr Coleridge has 'a mind reflecting ages past': his voice is like the echo of the congregated roar of the 'dark rearward and abyss' of thought . . .

This sonorous and perceptive opening stands prelude, in Hazlitt's essay, to the usual condescension, but it remains something like a rarity in its age among so many romantic disclaimers of literary tradition and indebtedness. Peacock too seems to have seen the truth in his *Four Ages of Poetry* (1820) but, perhaps facetiously, chose to misinterpret and exaggerate it: the poet, he wrote there, 'lives in the days that are past . . . The march of his intellect is like that of a crab, backwards.' Put in these paradoxical and patronizing terms, it stung Shelley into a passionate reply that denied it all and re-asserted the divinity of poetic inspiration. Perhaps Germany, on the whole, had more to offer than England in such matters, and German theorizing about poetry in the later eighteenth century seems to have had a boldness that the English lacked. 'To do the opposite,' as Lichtenberg put it in an aphorism of 1774-5, 'is also to imitate.' The German doctrine of 'romantic irony', as expounded by Friedrich Schlegel in 1797 and after, never quite succeeded in crossing the North Sea, and the phrase itself is an extreme rarity even in the Germany of that age. But it bears a family resemblance to Coleridge's exactly contemporary view of literary imitation: a doctrine of literary excellence that rejected the merely decorative flash of wit in favour of a diffusive humour pervading the entire course of a poem, a subtle and omnipresent egotism that worked through established literary forms in a perpetual consciousness of itself.

De Quincey, perhaps, reveals as much of an awareness of the broadening stream of literary precedent in his age as any English critic after Coleridge. The romantic model, he announced in a memorable essay on Jean Paul Richter in the *London Magazine* (December 1821), must henceforth be Germany rather than France, whose literature looks infertile and exhausted, being 'too intensely steeped in French manners to admit of any influences from without'. German literature, on the contrary, is youthful and alive, 'has most of a juvenile constitution', and Richter above all, in his novels, reveals a 'two-headed power . . . over the pathetic and the humorous'; or rather, a power 'not two-headed, but a one-headed Janus with two faces'. Poetic language, like language in general, he held to establish itself contextually in a rich infinity of modes that the old neoclassical system of the literary kinds was too crude to classify. De Quincey instances Mistress Quickly's speech on Falstaff's death in *Henry V* as a prime example of the Janus-faced —the solemn moment of a funereal panegyric enriched by the absurdities of a woman's ignorant and undisciplined affection:

> Nay, sure, he's not in hell: he's in Arthur's bosom, if ever man went to Arthur's bosom. A' made a finer end and went away an it had been any christom child . . . (II iii 8-10).

'How else could we have borne the jests of Sir Thomas More after his condemnation,' De Quincey goes on, 'which, as jests, would have been unseasonable from any body else; but, being felt in him to have a root in his character, they take the dignity of humorous traits, and do in fact deepen the pathos?'

But the great fund of knowledge of the imitative art in the England of that age lies in the poetry and criticism of Coleridge, exacting as it is to reach. The task, indeed, is doubly difficult: Coleridge's writings are only now becoming available in their entirety; and the imitative art, as a matter of theory at least, is in many ways remote from the interests of the present age. To an Englishman of the late eighteenth century, however, it is surely clear, it must have seemed the most natural of starting-points in any search for a doctrine of poetic creation.

# CHAPTER THREE

# Coleridge on Imitation

There are good reasons, then, for thinking that the English Romantics held a theory of literary kinds at least as ardently as the
Augustans had done, and that they practised it more consistently.
The case for supposing that they preferred the inchoate and the
fragmentary can hardly be made on the evidence, certainly, and
probably arises from a simple confusion of the English Romantics
with the Germans. Wordsworth, as late as the 1815 Preface, was
content with the traditional doctrine that there are 'laws and
appropriate graces of every species of composition', and listed seven
poetic forms, six of them classical and the seventh no more novel
than the 'composite order' of Young's *Night-Thoughts* and Cowper's *Task*. Coleridge often asserted his belief in the rightful
supremacy of the literary kinds. Such fragments as he did publish,
like 'Kubla Khan', are offered as incomplete attempts at writing
whole poems. On this subject he was often explicit. 'No work of
true genius,' as he said of Shakespeare in a late lecture, paraphrasing
A. W. Schlegel, 'dare want its appropriate form. . . As it must not,
neither can it, be lawless'—a judgment that leads into a defence of
'organic form' as 'innate' to the work itself: 'It shapes as it develops
itself from within, and the fullness of its development is one and the
same with the perfection of its outward form.'[1] Organic form,
evidently, will not finally content itself with the established modes.
But these modes are none the less the place to start, and the
romantic critic will find himself enlarging the range of possibilities
—by perceiving the individual nature of Shakespeare's formal

[1] Coleridge, *Shakespearean Crticism*, edited by T. M. Raysor, Cambridge, Mass.
(1930), vol i, pp. 223-4.

achievement, for example—rather than rejecting outright the system of categories he has inherited. Even those poets who are so great that they are 'above criticism', Coleridge wrote in a marginal note to Milton's poems, ought first to be subjected to the familiar discipline:

> speaking generally, it is far, far better to distinguish poetry into different classes, and instead of fault-finding, to say this belongs to such and such a class ... We may outgrow certain sorts of poetry (Young's *Night-Thoughts*, for instance) without arraigning their excellence *proprio genere* . . .

His remarks on Wordsworth's *Prelude* in *Table Talk* (21 July 1832), too, suggest that though the task of writing a great philosophical poem was bound to put some strain upon the system of established poetic categories, these categories were none the less essential as a starting-point. After a philosophical opening, he advised Wordsworth, the poet should 'describe the pastoral and other states of society, assuming something of the Juvenalian spirit as he approached the high civilization of cities and towns, and opening a melancholy picture of the present state of degeneracy and vice . . .', ending on a redemptive note. At first glance, this may look an unlikely programme for Wordsworth. But it may be recalled that Wordsworth's own classical interests were strong enough to approve, in principle at least, a proposal for a poem partly under Latin inspiration: he mentions in the *Recluse* (1888) how, like many Englishmen in the seventeenth and eighteenth centuries, he had aspired as a young man to write an epic:

> farewell
> That other hope, long mine, the hope to fill
> The heroic trumpet with the Muse's breath!

And the 'Laodamia' of 1814, an imitation of the sixth book of the *Aeneid*, as well as his abortive attempt in the 1820's to translate the whole *Aeneid* into heroic couplets, are evidences of the same bent. In any case, the *Prelude* of 1805—a poem still unpublished at the time Coleridge made his remark on its sequel—bears a

34

visible relationship to this edifying social programme, especially in its opening books, and still partly repays investigation in these terms.

The chief difficulty of discussing Coleridge's ideas on the making of poetry—theories which, in an enlarged sense of the word, I have called theories of imitation—is that they are inclined to involve themselves in the larger and more baffling question of the poet's relation to external reality: 'imitation in its largest sense', as Reynolds had put it. The poet imitates Nature, as European critics had known since Aristotle; he imitates its inward essence, according to a later refinement which Coleridge held, 'that which is within the thing' or its *natura naturans*.[2] I have powerful reasons for wishing to avoid this difficult issue here: partly because of its difficulty, partly because it is much discussed, and most of all because it threatens confusion with another, and for my present purpose more vital, use of the term. Imitation in its formal aspect, or the art of imitating other poems, is an issue that touches the quick of the poems themselves and helps to make sense of their variety of detail. No wonder if it figures so massively in Coleridge's own criticism. It represented for him the momentous paradox of language, and especially poetic language, as both a private and a public thing: private, being uniquely the work of its individual creator; and public, because itself a social inheritance understood by millions:

> Every man's language varies according to the extent of his know-
> ledge, the activity of his faculties and the depth or quickness of his
> feelings. Every man's language has, first, its individualities; secondly,
> the common properties of the class to which he belongs; and thirdly,
> words and phrases of universal use (*BL* xvii).

English, happily, is rich in association, in 'living words', having taken on the wealth of its own literary tradition. After all, language is 'the medium of all thoughts'; and nothing can be 'a medium in the living continuity of nature but by essentially partaking of the two things mediated' (*CN* 4,233). It is itself, then—a present fact;

[2] 'On Poetry or Art', or the thirteenth lecture of 1818; *Literary Remains*, edited by H. N. Coleridge, London (1836-9), vol. i, pp. 222, 225.

and it is also everything that has been memorably said in it. The poet's task is to make of this paradox a single thing, a 'unity in multeity' or 'harmonized chaos'. But no matter how original he may be, he can only use what he finds; he can 'only act through the intervention of articulate speech, which is so peculiarly human that in all languages it constitutes the ordinary phrase by which man and nature are contradistinguished'. The language of poetry, in fact, is a 'figured language', partaking at once of what it represents and of the humanity from which it is drawn.

To imitate a style, then, is by no means to reproduce it. 'The impression on the wax is not an imitation, but a copy, of the seal; the seal itself is an imitation.' The supreme function of poetic imitation is to be like and unlike at once: 'in all imitation two elements must coexist, and not only coexist, but must be perceived as coexisting. These two constitutent elements are likeness and unlikeness, or sameness and difference, and in all genuine creations of art there must be a union of these disparates.' An exact copy of the human is dull, even nauseating, since it omits 'the motion and the life' while yet adding 'every circumstance of detail'.[3] Mere mimicry, being only a copy, is damnable, and the talent for it 'strongest where the human race are most degraded', as among the Australian aborigines (*BL* iv n). In this view the business of the poet is not to copy but, at the highest, to contrast, to set off a poetic manner by using a model for a purpose which is not traditional but in which the traditional purpose yet remains apparent—as the 'Ancient Mariner', for example, continues to fulfil some of the functions of a medieval ballad and yet seems all the more modern for that reason. The best way to imitate, paradoxically, is to oppose, and so the poet's duty may even lie in choosing the most challenging and least congruous materials in which to work. 'EXTREMES MEET', as he wrote in large letters in a notebook in December 1803, and went on: 'a perfectly unheard-of subject, and a *crambe bis cocta* chosen by a man of genius—difficult to say which would excite in the higher degree the sense of novelty' (*CN* 1,725); and he regretted he had not made a collection of instances of literary paradox from

[3] *Literary Remains*, i, 218-30.

high and low, quoting Milton's 'The parching air / Burns frore . . .'
and 'Dark with excess of light.' A few years later he planned an
essay on 'the Like in the Unlike' (*CN* 3,395); and he seems to have
believed with especial emphasis that it was the supreme mark of
promise in a young poet to choose subjects alien to his personal
interests, beginning with 'things remote from his own feelings'—
things 'in which the romanticity gives a vividness to the naturalness
of the sentiments and feelings' (*CN* 3,247). 'Romanticity', evidently,
a word of rare occurrence in English, here signifies the principle
of artistic remoteness itself.

The extremes that meet in Coleridge's poetry are extremes of
past and present. His most characteristic contribution to our knowledge of literature lies directly here, in his grasp of the paradox of
a present past. The time-dimension, it is true, is an intensifying
factor in English poetry in the seventeenth and eighteenth centuries;
but in Coleridge the dimension is exceptionally full in its variety
and perhaps unique in its deliberation. His own age seems to have
had more than an inkling of this, though it has since passed out of
the currency of literary history—so much so that it is possible to
hear a similar doctrine of literary tradition discussed as being
among the discoveries of T. S. Eliot in the 1920's. A younger contemporary, shortly before Coleridge died, spoke of him as the
accepted parent of 'our (modern) romantic poetry', and described
the effect of Percy's *Reliques* as 'a latent suspicion of the value of
re-working forgotten mines'.[4] It is not surprising if Coleridge
handled Wordsworth's jejune theories of poetic language with such
aplomb in the later chapters of the *Biographia Literaria*. The Wordsworthian notions of a broad similarity between the language of
poetry and of prose, or between prose and ordinary conversation,
fall swiftly under the arguments of a practised advocate of poetic
ventriloquism, of the conscious choice of past styles. His appeal to
passages from Chaucer's *Troilus and Criseyde* and Herbert's *Temple*
(*BL* xix) have deepened forever the awareness of the English poet
that literary history is his business too, that dead ages can be put
to lively uses.

[4] Edward Lytton Bulwer (1803-1873), *England and the English*, Paris (1833), pp. 287,
288n.

This is a principle which Coleridge conceived, at the latest, nearly two years before he encouraged Wordsworth to write the contentious Preface of 1800. In a letter to Wordsworth himself (January 1798) he expressed his surprise at Monk Lewis for introducing 'a pretty little ballad-song' into a play, *Castle Spectre*. 'The simplicity and naturalness is his own, and not imitated; for it is made to subsist in congruity with a language perfectly modern—the language of his own times, in the same way that the language of the writer of 'Sir Cauline' [in Percy's *Reliques*] was the language of *his* times'. Coleridge went on to explain how his own gift, at the very moment when he was at the height of his poetic activity, differed from Lewis's strange independence of ancient sources: 'I find *I* cannot attain this innocent nakedness except by *assumption*—I resemble the Duchess of Kingston, who masqueraded in the character of "Eve before the Fall" in flesh-coloured silk' (*CL* i 379). He needed such meetings of extreme with extreme, 'the balance and reconciliation of opposite or discordant qualities; . . . the sense of novelty and freshness, with old and familiar objects' (*BL* xiv). He knew that he needed not one language, but many: all the arts of ventriloquism, as he often called it, or the arts of mediating his poetic gift through the forms of others. Only those who lack originality, he believed with Blake, avoid plagiarism and imitation: the truly original poet embraces it, and glories in the poetic heritage waiting to be used: 'the certainty and feeling [of originality] is enough . . . and he rejoices to find his opinions plumed and winged with the authority of venerable forefathers' (*CN* 1,695). Some men of genius, especially philosophers, he thought to have been ensnared by the temptation to coin a language of their own—'a strong feeling of originality seems to receive a gratification by new terms' (*CN* 1,835)—whereas the greatest poetry, like Chaucer's, astonishingly survives the shift of language by the weight of its own excellence, and demands to live by its own right. Plagiarism, in this view, is not so much a poet's right as his duty. The poet does not make new things, but makes things new. 'The Eighth Commandment was not made for Bards,' he facetiously concluded 'The Reproof and Reply' (*CPW* 443), a nonsense-poem written as an apology for having stolen some flowers from a friend's garden. Bound as the poet is to start with language as he finds it, he ought, as a start, to accept the fact. The peril is that he should otherwise behave as Wordsworth had appeared to advocate in the 1800 Preface, dogmatically evicting 'poetic diction', or the accepted language of English poetry, avoiding the hackneyed like the plague, and supposing too readily that the language he hears about him in conversation is, after some selection, a sufficient model. In fact the poet needs the past: it is a blessing, not an imposition. In any case, what is and is not hackneyed is a relative rather than an absolute matter, 'dependent on the age in which the author wrote and not deduced from the nature of the thing' (*BL* xviii). A past, it is true, can grow too old for us, can wear itself out, like the 'exploded mythology' of the Ancients in our Renaissance poetry. But another past, a new past, can still strike clear and fresh. A language may even, like Italian at the time of Dante, achieve classical form too soon, a matter of sheer bad luck for those who follow after. In that case the poet may find the limitation crippling: 'The mind catching at a new intuition will be impeded by its want of a verbal symbol, paralysed by its not daring (in that formed state of language) to invent or rather generate a symbol representative of the intuition'; he may even feel 'tempted to corrupt and alloy the purity of the new intuition by the attempt to express it by some false analogy through some former symbol' (*CN* 3,946). Simply because poetic excellence is a fact of the historical moment, the poet needs to be lucky in his time and place.

All this should not be allowed to suggest that Coleridge's curiosity about the historical past was limitless. Oddly enough, there is a special sense in which he was hardly interested in history at all. He seems to have been one of those whose passion for the past is quite independent of anything like a professional historian's grasp of detail. Like Dr Johnson, he would probably have been bored stiff by a conversation about the Punic Wars. His favourite studies, as he confessed in a letter of November 1796, were 'metaphysics, and poetry, and "facts of mind"': 'I have read and digested most of the historical writers—but I do not *like* history' (*CL* i 260). In spite of his enthusiasm for the idea of 'the Gothic', he was not in the least interested in actual medieval churches, and there is a story how on a visit to York he once got as far as the entrance to the Minster without bothering to enter it. On returning from Rome in 1806 a friend remembered his describing 'the state of society; the characters of the Pope and Cardinals; the gorgeous ceremonies, with the superstitions of the people, but not one word did he utter concerning St Peter's, the Vatican, or the numerous *antiquities* of the place'.[5] Association bored him too: he once mockingly boasted a total lack of interest in Shakespeare's mulberry tree and the Plain of Marathon. His intelligence was conceptual, and particularities only found a place there if his ideas could find a place for them; they could serve as examples or they could go. In many ways, in fact, he saw the past as other late eighteenth-century Englishmen had done, if with greater passion and exuberance. He inherited the literary imitation of the medieval ballad, for example, from Percy and Scott. His review, as a twenty-one-year-old, of Mrs Radcliffe's *Mysteries of Udolpho* in the *Critical Review* (August 1794), if indeed it is Coleridge's, would suggest how incuriously (from an historian's point of view) he may have accepted the conventions of the Gothic novel which had come into vogue in his childhood. Protesting against the medieval heroine's excessive gentility, the reviewer argued that though perhaps there was 'no direct anachronism' in it, yet such lady-like accomplishments 'give so much the air of modern manners as is not counterbalanced by Gothic arches and antique furniture'; and the review continued:

> It is possible that the manners of different ages may not differ so much as we are apt to imagine, and more than probable that we are generally wrong when we attempt to delineate any but our own; but there is at least a style of manners which our imagination has appropriated to each period, and which, like the costume of theatrical dress, is not departed from without hurting the feelings.

Literary convention, in fact, is much more important than historical accuracy—for a poet, a sternly and reasonably businesslike view, and very like the Augustan one. If Coleridge suspected the eighteenth century, it was not because he did not belong to it, but rather because in so many significant respects he did. It was too near, too

[5] Joseph Cottle, *Reminiscences of Coleridge and Southey*, London (1847), pp. 313-14n.

like himself; it violated the principle of 'assumption'. It was so easy and natural to imitate that imitation lost its force:

> Every one of tolerable education feels the *imitability* of Dr Johnson's and other such's style, the inimitability of Shakespeare etc. Hence, I believe, arises the partiality of thousands to Johnson: they can imagine themselves doing the same. Vanity is at the bottom of it. The number of imitators proves this in some measure (*CN* 2,407).

It was to 'the spiritual Platonic old England' of Sidney, Shakespeare, Spenser, Milton, Bacon, Swift and Wordsworth (*CN* 2,598) that, by 1805, he felt an English poet must turn, as he should turn away from the 'commercial Gt Britain' of Paley, Hayley and Erasmus Darwin, 'with Locke at the head of the philosophers and Pope of the poets'. The choice involved an injustice to Augustan poetry, but it was still necessary. A man cannot put on his own skin, or assume what he already is. That 'certain aloofness'[6] which, by the turn of the century, he had come to see that the language of poetry demanded could not drive him back to the language of the Augustans, which stood too near too look interesting. In any case, to imitate a modern poem is either to fall into the merely commonplace or, if the imitation has an edge to it, to make fun. It is only the imitation of the remote that dignifies either the chosen model or itself. 'Parodies on new poems are read as satires; on old ones (the soliloquy of Hamlet for instance) as compliments.'[7] This is why the poet, in the long run, has nothing to fear from parody, which 'in half a century or less' turns into an encomium anyhow. A poet can even afford to parody himself, as Coleridge did in the last of the three sonnets published under the pseudonym of Nehemiah Higginbottom in the *Monthly Magazine* of November 1797, written at the height of his activity as a poet:

> And this reft house is that, the which he built,
> Lamented Jack! . . .

a parody undertaken, as he explained years later, to laugh himself out of 'the indiscriminate use of elaborate and swelling language

---

[6] Letter to Thomas Wedgwood, 20 October 1802; *CL* ii 877.
[7] *Omniana*, London (1812), no. 105.

and imagery' (*BL* i). And certainly these 'Sonnets Attempted in the Manner of Contemporary Writers' (*CPW* 209-11), written to expose certain abuses in the poems of Lamb and Charles Lloyd, as well as his own, are calculated in their good humour to hurt nobody.

For nearly half a century, as a poet, he paid to many the reverent or mocking compliment of imitation: to Anacreon, Horace, Ossian, Bowles and others in his youth; to the medieval ballad; to Cowper in the conversation-poems; to Skelton, Shakespeare, Fulke Greville, Milton, Pope, Akenside, Schiller. . . . In a letter of July 1821, summing up a career not far from its close, he called poets 'a very chameleonic race: they take the colour not only of what they feed on, but of the very leaves under which they pass'. Facetious or solemn, his mind ran in fascination upon literary convention and literary models, apt and inapt, great and small. 'If I felt any real anger,' he wrote indignantly in a letter of 12 September 1814 against those who called him lazy, 'I should not do what I fully intend to do, publish two long satires in Drydenic verse, entitled *Puff* and *Slander*' (*CL* iii 532)—feeling perhaps that a bout of pastiche is a good cure for the sulks, which perhaps it is. The greatest matter here for wonder lies in his abundance, in the rich simultaneity of his poetic impulses. 'The Ancient Mariner', 'Frost at Midnight', and 'France: an Ode' are three poems written within a few months of one another, in the winter of 1797-8—the first an imitation of the medieval ballad, the second of Cowper, the third of the Pindaric ode. The sameness of the eighteenth century, as he saw it, was a challenge: it was there to be shattered. 'What should we think of music, if all airs were composed to the tune of "God Save the King" and "Rule Britannia"? Yet this is not a very unfair statement of the truth respecting our style since the writings of Johnson, Junius and the Scotch translators of their thoughts into English' (*CN* 3,655). It is not that there is anything new in the notion of a poet looking backwards for the inspiration of diversity. The ancient world, after all, had proclaimed Mnemosyne, Goddess of Memory, as mother of the Muses. But the Romantics seem to have regarded the past in a spirit of something like intoxication. At the close of *Hyperion*, at the moment when Mnemosyne is about to deify him, Apollo reads in her face the 'wondrous lesson' of the new poetry of which Keats was both the prophet and the source:

> Knowledge enormous makes a God of me.
> Names, deeds, grey legends, dire events, rebellions,
> Majesties, sovran voices, agonies,
> Creations and destroyings, all at once
> Pour into the wide hollows of my brain . . .

The evidence here is likely to prove abundant to the point of embarrassment. The best thread through the labyrinth, perhaps, lies in Coleridge's own critical consciousness of what he is doing, and in the fact of which he was himself so deeply aware: that his own poetry never seems so much itself as when it is pretending to be something else. 'When a man is attempting to describe another's character,' as he once put it, 'in one thing he will always succeed: in describing himself' (*CN* 74). In examining the models that he used, there is no danger of discovering in the end anyone but STC.

# THE POEMS

# CHAPTER FOUR

# Youth and the Drama

One good compliment to pay a poet, at the outset, is not to linger over his juvenilia. But Coleridge's early poems deserve something more than a glance, if only because they are his; and his plays cannot altogether be left out of the account, even if they demonstrate that his talent for the drama was nearly nothing. I associate the two here as a matter of convenience, though the dramatic attempts continue well into middle age, in the hope that the revelations they offer, however desultory, may justify themselves by accumulation.

Coleridge began writing poetry at least as early as the age of fourteen ('Easter Holidays', *CPW* 1) and began publishing at seventeen ('The Abode of Love'),[1] while he was still a schoolboy at Christ's Hospital. About a dozen poems dating from before his undergraduate days at Jesus College Cambridge (1791-4) have survived. It seems natural now to expect that so young a poet would begin with naïve, unconscious imitation of his elders, and only slowly discover the delights of deliberate imitation. But this would be to misunderstand the nature of education in that age: both Wordsworth's and Coleridge's surviving schoolboy poems are largely deliberate imitations of classical models, and they include parodies as well as reverential imitations from the start. There is a great deal of boyish solemnity in 'Dura Navis', a Horatian exercise of 1787; and the first draft of the declamatory 'Monody on the Death of Chatterton', written in 1790 in the Golden Book of his schoolmaster Bowyer, is an extravagant and humourless attempt at writing a Pindaric ode which Coleridge was to revise six times

---

[1] Published in the *London World* (26 July 1790) and in the *Cambridge Chronicle* five days later.

during the next forty years, to end as a bitter elegy in riming couplets. But 'Devonshire Roads' is a parody of *Paradise Lost*, at once cutting and affectionate—or rather, of eighteenth-century Miltonics—in the form of a 'furious ode':

> When the sad fiends thro' Hell's sulphureous roads
> Took the first survey of their new abodes;
> Or when the fall'n Archangel fierce
> Dar'd through the realms of Night to pierce,
> What time the Bloodhound lur'd by human scent
> Thro' all Confusion's quagmires floundering went.
> *(CPW* 27).

and the riotous 'Mathematical Problem', a geometrical Pindaric, was sent to his brother from Christ's Hospital, claiming to be the first of a series of odes which would translate the whole of Euclid. Any liberties it committed, wrote the eighteen-year-old poet, were 'equally homogeneal with the exactness of mathematical disquisition and the boldness of Pindaric daring' *(CL* i 7). The seeming gravity of the farewell ode on leaving school for Cambridge, 'Absence', published in the *Cambridge Intelligencer* in October 1794, is belied by what appears to be its earlier version in a letter of April 1792, which openly betrays itself as an Augustan parody:

> Where deep in mud Cam rolls his slumbrous stream,
> And Bog and Desolation reign supreme,
> Where all Boeotia clouds the misty brain,
> The Owl Mathesis pipes her loathsome strain . . . *(CL* i 34).

Mathesis, or education, never attracted Coleridge much in its formal aspects, and his university career was inglorious; but in the published version the poem turns as respectable (in both senses) as this:

> Where graced with many a classic spoil
> Cam rolls his reverend stream along,
> I haste to urge the learned toil
> That sternly chides my love-lorn song . . . *(CPW* 29).

If the earlier letter had not survived, we should certainly have committed the usual mistake of supposing 'Absence' to be further evidence for Coleridge's laborious solemnity. In fact some jokes, like the 'Monody on a Tea-Kettle' (*CPW* 18), give themselves away at a glance; others are occult. Not many readers (in this century, at least) would notice that the Cambridge poem 'Inside the Coach' (*CPW* 26-7), a comic poem on the difficulties of sleeping on a journey, parodies the opening lines of Dyer's *Grongar Hill* (1726):

> Slumbrous God of half-shut eye!
> Who lovest with limbs supine to lie . . .
>
> (Silent nymph, with curious eye!
> Who, the purple evening, lie . . .)

Indeed the comic and esoteric aspects of Coleridge's early genius were carefully under-emphasized in his first collection, *Poems on Various Subjects*, published in Bristol in 1796, as they have been under-emphasized ever since. This is the year in which the fructifying and agonizing friendship with Wordsworth began, so that the 1796 volume conveniently represents the trend of his poetic talent before the advent of that masterly but inconsiderate collaborator. The 1796 poems are broadly of two kinds. First, there are the more numerous poems which Coleridge often calls 'monodies' or, more often, 'effusions'—private outpourings which could sometimes be confined, after the manner of Bowles's sonnets of 1789, to a fourteen-liner, or which might as easily ramble into blank verse. The great conversation-poems of the middle years, such as 'Frost at Midnight', find their origins here. Considered together, they are the poems Coleridge apologizes for in his 1796 preface, poems of a 'querulous egotism'; such egotism would be out of place in an historical or epic poem, Coleridge argues engagingly, but 'to censure it in a Monody or Sonnet is almost as absurd as to dislike a circle for being round' (*CPW* 1135-6). And secondly, there are the odes, where Coleridge's genius and the late Augustan are most fatally at one: such as the 'Monody on the Death of Chatterton' (an ode in spite of its title), extensively revised for the 1796 volume (*CPW* 125-31)—a poem on the poetic vocation which Coleridge later claimed to have begun at the age of twelve (*CL* iv 937n); or the

'Ode to the Departing Year' of 1796, which strikes, with altogether too much conviction, the full tone of Gray in its very opening:

> Spirit who sweepest the wild Harp of Time! (*CPW* 160).

Coleridge was to record only two triumphs in a form so uncomfortably close in time to his own age. First came 'France: an Ode', which appeared in the *Morning Post* in April 1798 to rebuke revolutionary France for her unprovoked invasion of Switzerland:

> To mix with Kings in the low lust of sway,
> Yell in the hunt, and share the murderous prey (*CPW* 246).

It is a poem that offers a good deal of excited and vigorous political verse. But excitement needs to be tamed to make a poem, and the final stanza achieves only a kind of licentious confusion:

> The Sensual and the Dark rebel in vain,
> Slaves by their own compulsion! In mad game
> They burst their manacles and wear the name
> Of Freedom, graven on a heavier chain!

Moral indignation serves Coleridge badly at such moments, and the 'wild Pindaric' does not offer him the encouragement to master it. The second triumph, the Dejection Ode of 1802, is more characteristic and more complex, and must await a later discussion. But it is notable that both 'France' and 'Dejection' fall outside the net of Coleridge's early collections of 1796, 1797 and 1803. They are occasional, improbable, and ambiguous victories in a poetic mode which no talent, one may suspect, could at so late a date readily subdue into any kind of intelligent decorum.

Indiscipline, indeed, and especially an exclamatory indiscipline, is the besetting sin of Coleridge's early poems. They excel when most humorous and seemingly most casual, as in the conversation-poems, where the simple ease which thousands of Englishmen since Shakespeare and Milton have shown in writing blank verse—in talking it, one is almost inclined to say—makes for its own quiet, allusive self-control. They founder most disastrously when most ambitious. 'Religious Musings', a vast blank verse monody of

1794-6 expressive of Coleridge's early unitarian enthusiasm, is a disastrous example:

> There is one Mind, one omnipresent Mind,
> Omnific. His most holy name is Love.
> Truth of subliming import! . . . (*CPW* 113).

The appalling 'Destiny of Nations'—nearly five hundred lines of grotesquely Miltonic blank verse—seems to have been written in 1796 too, when much of it appeared in Southey's *Joan of Arc*, though it was not published complete until the *Sibylline Leaves* of 1817. The highminded balderdash of these two poems might almost have sunk the volumes they overburdened, and they alert the reader still to a threat of unforgivable tedium.

But it is the effusion that dominates these early volumes, the 'querulous egotism' that is openly the subject of most of the poems and which invades even those where it has no place. Coleridge, in the 1796 preface, evidently thought it a somewhat novel form. It is certainly not Wordsworthian: Coleridge wrote practically all the 1796 poems before he knew Wordsworth in any sense that counted, and though Wordsworth's early publications, *An Evening Walk* (1793) and *Descriptive Sketches* (1793), were effusive too, Coleridge had no need to turn to them. The name of the Reverend William Lisle Bowles (1762-1850)—the source Coleridge hailed, in the first chapter of the *Biographia*, as his schoolboy inspiration—strikes no chord today, and need strike none, since what Coleridge found in Bowles's twenty-one sentimental sonnets of 1789 he could surely have found as well, and better, in Gray, Collins and Cowper. What a sixteen-year-old schoolboy reads and enthuses over with his friends is so much a matter of accident that the issue needs to be pressed no further. Bowles, a Man of Sensibility in the character of the sonneteer, touched a nerve in Coleridge that many another might have touched as well. I make no attempt to revive his memory here, but certain calumnies need to be disposed of. Bowles's talent was sentimental and thin, but in saying just that we exculpate him from the charge of perverting the genius of his great disciple. Coleridge's worst sins as a young poet were not his. He was not exclamatory, and he was not embarrassingly cosmic in his aspirations. He can hardly have encouraged Coleridge to attempt either 'Religious Musings' or 'The Destiny of Nations'. In his taste for nostalgia—for the intimate, private relations of object, place, and moment, of a sort which Wordsworth later explored in depth— he helpfully anticipates a mode in which Coleridge in the mid 1790's began to excel. And he is not a dangerously ornate poet: his language is the language of such late Augustans as Gray and Collins in weak dilution. That language, as Coleridge knew, was itself something of a model in directness and simplicity, and one that could teach him something he often found hard to learn. In the 1797 preface, where he writes of having 'pruned the double-epithets with no sparing hand and used my best efforts to tame the swell and glitter both of thought and diction,' he speaks of Gray and Collins as justly established reputations. If the tradition of Pope had divided in mid-century between the plain and the ornate, be- tween Collins and Erasmus Darwin, then much of Coleridge's early poetry is a battle-ground on which this unresolved quarrel is fought out. Head and heart were hardly at one, but Bowles surely helped him, on balance, to apply the rough, deflating advice of his schoolmaster Bowyer to his own exuberance ('Muse, boy, muse? Your nurse's daughter, you mean!') He humbly accepted the stric- tures of a friend on the 'rage and affectation of double epithets' in the poems of 1796 (*CL* i 215), came to see that the profound defect of contemporary poetry was its 'anxiety to be always striking' (*CN* 2,728) and—but by now the slight example of Bowles could neither help nor hinder him—settled in middle age, in theory at least, upon that 'neutral style' which he claimed to find in Chaucer's *Troilus* and in Herbert's Temple (*BL* xix).

The true function of Bowles as a stepping-stone on which Cole- ridge's youthful talent rose can best be seen in an evolving attitude to moral sentiments. In the preface to *A Sheet of Sonnets* (1796), a pamphlet of twenty-eight sonnets to be bound up with Bowles's, all Coleridge's praise goes to poems 'in which moral sentiments, affections, or feelings, are deduced from, and associated with, the scenery of Nature' (*CPW* 1,139). Six years later, in a letter to Sotheby, Bowles's later poems are damned for their 'perpetual trick of *moralizing* every thing'. Coleridge goes on:

Never to see or describe any interesting appearance in nature, without connecting it by dim analogies with the moral world, proves faintness of impression. Nature has her proper interest; and he will know what it is, who believes and feels that every thing has a life of its own, and that we are all *one life*. A poet's heart and intellect should be combined, intimately combined and unified, with the great appearances in Nature—and not merely held in solution and loose mixture with them, in the shape of formal similes . . . Bowles has indeed the sensibility of a poet; but he has not the passion of a great poet  (*CL* ii 864).

The vulgar error that the English Romantics revived the poet's interest in natural objects is deftly exposed here, for what Coleridge offers is the characteristic recall of his age to the human condition as the poet's true theme: 'the mind of man,' as Wordsworth put it at the end of the poem he wrote for his friend, which is 'a thousand times more beautiful than the earth On which he dwells'.[2] After the poetry of natural sentiment, this new and vital doctrine of a poetry of humanity must have tasted like claret after weak tea, and it decisively marks an end, around the turn of the century, to Coleridge's poetic youth.

Coleridge's attempt to turn himself into a dramatist, on the other hand, lasted into late middle age, but the oddity that he alone among the English romantic poets achieved a successful run on the London stage ought not to disguise the fact of total failure. In the drama Coleridge achieved neither artistic distinction nor a source of income. And he knew it. 'To have conceived strongly,' as he put it in the preface to *Osorio*, 'does not always imply the power of successful execution' (*CPW* 1,114). The harvest was two plays, the *Osorio* of 1797 (radically revised in 1813 as *Remorse*) and the *Zapolya* of 1816, a feeble imitation of Shakespeare's *Winter's Tale*, as well as two Schiller versions and three dramatic fragments; and of these only the translations from the German are fully significant.

The failure of the Romantics, and of the Victorian poets, to create a drama has been earnestly debated. But it is important to realize at the outset that in England at least what was attempted was scarcely a romantic drama at all. Most ambitious plays of the

[2] *The Prelude* (1805 version), xiii 446-8.

Regency, including Coleridge's and Byron's, are heroic dramas in direct descent from Corneille and Dryden. In language and metre they may ape the Jacobeans, but in plot and in moral assumptions they are in the direct and continuous theatrical tradition of the world of Almanzor. It is not so much that romantic drama was attempted unsuccessfully as that it was not attempted at all. The romantic features are incidental. Characters move puppet-like upon familiar, absolute principles such as the point of honour and the conflict between love and duty, with poetic justice descending suddenly in the fifth act. Death falls upon a mark of exclamation. Finesse of motive is unattainable, even inconceivable, in such a world. Both place and time of action are deliberately remote, and yet remoteness is rarely put to romantic effect. These plays simply do not belong to their age as do the poems and novels of the Regency. They are late, insignificant vestiges of a decaying literary form. Failure, or at the best mediocrity, is implicit in the undertaking itself. One radical consideration forbade success. Early romantic poetry lacked a fixed audience of any kind, and only gradually, though with surprising rapidity, made the world of sensibility by which its work was enjoyed. And the drama demands an audience which is visible and immediate. It is not surprising if the romantic poets, whose chief motive for writing plays was commonly financial, shunned in drama all thoughts of the experimental.

Coleridge made his first dramatic attempt at the age of twenty-one, when in a few weeks he composed the first act of *The Fall of Robespierre*, Southey writing the second and third. It was a work of immense topicality. Robespierre, who had violated all the liberal hopes of English admirers of the Revolution, had been guillotined on 28th July 1794. The *Morning Chronicle* confirmed the rumour from a France at war on 18th August, printing Robespierre's last speeches, and Coleridge seems to have written his act in the course of that month, recreating the world of contemporary France in English blank verse from newspaper reports. Such immediacy of response might seem to promise a new drama; in fact it only confirms the old. 'The empassioned and highly figurative language of the French orators,' as Coleridge called it, was taken as an open excuse to indulge a taste for the exclamatory. The moral absolutism of Pantisocracy, in which Coleridge and Southey still believed, with its youthful object of making men 'necessarily virtuous by removing all motives to evil' (*CL* i 114), fitted much too neatly the stoic virtues of heroic tragedy, where the moral absolutism of human self-sufficiency offered easy models for attitudinizing. This first failure is confirmed in *Osorio*, written three years later at Sheridan's suggestion, refused by Drury Lane in December 1797 on grounds of obscurity, and revised sixteen years after. Its plot, which is sent in sixteenth-century Spain, offers no more than the interest of a story of senseless injury which, like the Ancient Mariner's, is followed by repentance. But here, in the corrupted frame of heroic tragedy, it offers emotional vulgarity as well:

Forgive me, Albert!—*Curse* me with forgiveness (*CPW* 594).

Written, as Coleridge later admitted, in ignorance of 'all stage-tactics' (*CPW* 812), *Osorio* was turned in 1813 into the more efficient vehicle of *Remorse*, with the help of the manager of Drury Lane, and ran there for twenty nights. No one could wish to see it revived.

The same verdict cannot be pronounced over the versions of Schiller's *Die Piccolomini* and *Wallensteins Tod*, plays which Coleridge translated at high speed shortly after his return from Germany, between December 1799 and April 1800, from copies supplied by the publisher Longmans and attested by the hand of Schiller himself. The plays came hot from the creator's hand—a vast tragedy in ten acts begun by Schiller in 1796 and preceded by a one-act introduction, *Wallensteins Lager*, which Coleridge omitted as superfluous. With all due reservation concerning detail, Coleridge's *Wallenstein* deserves to rank among the climactic examples of English poetic translation, though English immunity in this century to the genius of the greatest German tragedian will probably continue to keep it off the London stage. Coleridge's view of Schiller was the view of his age: he had been bowled over by *Die Räuber* as a Cambridge undergraduate in 1794, and his knowledge of German, it is now clear, was already considerable before he set out for Germany with Wordsworth in 1798. He was the first great

English author for whom German, rather than French or Latin, was the chief point of entry into continental civilization. The *Wallenstein* confirms this view: Coleridge omits and dilates, but his misunderstandings are not numerous for a work of such scale. His unfulfilled version of Part I of Goethe's *Faust,* which he seems to have promised to translate for John Murray in 1814, must have been well within his range; 'no one but Coleridge' as Shelley wrote in a letter of April 1822, 'is capable of this work.'

The fascination of Coleridge's *Wallenstein* lies in the spectacle of one great poet at work upon another with a third, Shakespeare, holding varying sway over them both. The German originals were already Shakespearean, and to an extent that German audiences have perhaps seldom realized. The world of haughty, and yet bitingly argumentative, debate and intrigue among the great ones of a national past, and in an age of civil war, interspersed with humorous prose scenes allotted to their menials, reminds the English reader irresistibly of Shakespeare's histories, and the striking inter-relation between the public pretensions and private weaknesses of Schiller's soldiers and noblemen of the Thirty Years War reminds the English reader of *Julius Caesar* too. The heroic and deluded figure of Wallenstein himself, buoyed up by a faith in astrology into a conviction that, in deserting the Emperor for the Protestant cause, he can carry his army with him into the Swedish camp, succeeds in real measure in establishing itself, much as Shakespeare's Brutus does, in the double role of public hero and private conscience. Schiller had isolated and intensified the problem with something like Shakespeare's eye for the dramatic chance: 'I am purposely seeking for limitation in the historical sources,' he wrote to Körner, 'in order that my ideas may be strictly determined and realized by surrounding circumstance.' The notion of determining by selected circumstance is one that must have fallen aptly upon a Coleridge fresh from a visit to Germany itself, the great source and origin in that age, as De Quincey later saw, of an historical awareness in poetry. The contrast with what French drama had to offer in 1800 is decisive: France might have taught him heroic drama, but in serious theatre it could teach him nothing better. *Wallenstein* is a play of intrigue set against a realized, and consciously limited, background of seventeenth-century Germany, a play of minutely shifting political and personal relations—relations which shift as far as a point of reversal so that, at the close, Wallenstein is murdered by one of his own followers—and where the tragedy of the direct and idealistic young Max Piccolomini sets off the true nature of a world where a man must intrigue or die. In one large regard only, the play remains stubbornly un-Shakespearean—in its explicitness. It belongs damagingly to an age in European drama where the simplest actions performed before the eyes of the audience still need to be reported by some bystander ('He dies'); and grandiose as it is, it remains in its details something of a test to the patience of another age.

Coleridge found a modern Shakespearean play and shakespearean-ized it more. His preface calls the translation a literal one, 'wherever I was not prevented by absolute differences of idiom' (*CPW* 599), but this is a licence almost infinite in its extension. Coleridge seems to have been aware of the embarrassingly large English shadow that lies across the German, and in a manuscript note he knowingly convicted Schiller of one 'most egregious misimitation of Shakes-peare', in the ludicrous talk that he attributes to his murderers (*CPW* 599). And yet he recogizes that the Shakespeare in question is not, fortunately, that of *Lear* or *Othello*, but rather the less dis-ciplined world of *Richard II* or *Henry VI*. History is less tidy than tragedy: 'We scarcely expect rapidity in an Historical Drama; and many prolix speeches are pardoned from characters whose names and actions have formed the most amusing tales of our early life' (*CPW* 725). The presence of Shakespeare is not most easily demon-strated by individual passages, since it is a kind of omnipresence of word, action, and atmosphere; but one or two passages may serve. Isolani, Wallenstein's Croat general, is complaining of his treatment as a plain soldier seeking supplies at the Emperor's court:

> . . . How from one antechamber to another
> They dragged me on, and left me by the hour
> To kick my heels among a crowd of simpering
> Feast-fattened slaves . . . And, at last,
> Whom should they send me but a Capuchin . . .
>
> (*CPW* 606).

57

In this instance the resemblance to Hotspur's speech to the King in the third scene of *1 Henry IV* ('My liege, I did deny no prisoners . . .') is compelling only in general terms—here there are no close verbal parallels. But Illo's speech later in the first act of *The Piccolomini*, like many other sententious passages in the *Wallenstein*, echoes faintly but distinctly a greater poet:

> Seize, seize the hour
> Ere it slips from you . . .
> 'Tis the high tide that heaves the stranded ship . . . (*CPW* 628-9).

behind which dimly sounds Brutus's speech before Philippi in *Julius Caesar* (IV iii):

> There is a tide in the affairs of men . . .

Admittedly not all of Coleridge's intensifications of the Shakespearean element are happy. The insertion of

> I see the youth, in my mind's eye I see him   (*CPW* 601).

a phrase snatched from *Hamlet* which bears no equivalence in the original German, hardly contributes to our picture of Isolani as a bluff and honest soldier. And

> The neighing war-horse, the air-shattering trumpet   (*CPW* 614).

is a line which, in itself, is not grossly out of character with the young and ardent Max; but its proximity to the outcry of the embittered Othello is unhelpful:

> Farewell the neighing steed, and the shrill trump   (III iii).

And yet, with few exceptions, the plays are best when most Shakespearean. The merely 'romantic' passages, written in an idiom peculiar to the age of Schiller and Coleridge, are commonly feeble —like the recollection by a friend of what the young Wallenstein was like, pronounced just before his murder:

> Yet even then he had a daring soul;
> His frame of mind was serious and severe
> Beyond his years: his dreams were of great objects.

He was led amidst us of a silent spirit
Communing with himself . . (*CPW* 767).

It is not at such moments as these that the drama is memorable, but rather at those in which it attempts, in the fullest audacity, to evoke a dead age by brilliantly selected detail. Thekla, for example, describes what she saw in the tower where her father, Wallenstein, indulges his passion for astrology:

Here six or seven
Colossal statues, and all kings, stood round me
In a half-circle. Each one in his hand
A sceptre bore, and on his head a star . . .
And this was Jupiter, my father's star;
And at his side I saw the Sun and Moon  (*CPW* 648).

Here, and at similar moments, the compromise with history that is called romanticism finds definition and embodiment. The reply made by her lover Max, indeed, might serve as a motto to the work of Coleridge's life:

The intelligible forms of ancient poets,
The fair humanities of old religion,
The power, the beauty, and the majesty
That had their haunts in dale, or piny mountain,
Or forest by slow stream, or pebbly spring,
Or chasms and wat'ry depths; all these have vanished.
They live no longer in the faith of reason!
But still the heart doth need a language, still
Doth the old instinct bring back the old names . . . (*CPW* 649).

Schiller has embodied in Wallenstein's infatuation with astrology the yearnings of a whole generation of Europeans to reclaim the past in order to solve the dilemma of the present age; his tactic is deliberately to choose an absurdity such as astrology and defy 'the faith of reason' to laugh at it. It is the measure of his dramatic success, and of Coleridge's, that the remote and implausible heroism of Wallenstein, though erroneous in all its hopes and convictions, still sounds through the tragedy with the clarity of one who speaks for a new age.

# CHAPTER FIVE

# The Conversation Poems

In the course of 1795, at the age of twenty-two and in the year of
his marriage, Coleridge invented the only poetic form he was ever
to invent—the 'conversational poem', to adopt his subtitle to 'The
Nightingale' in *Lyrical Ballads*, or the 'conversation poem', as it
was to become in *Sibylline Leaves* (1817). The name is both convenient and misleading. A conversation is an exchange; and these
poems, a dozen or fewer, stretching from 'The Eolian Harp' in
August 1795 as far as 'To William Wordsworth' in January 1807,
and perhaps further, are plainly monologues. Those who met
Coleridge in his later life, it is true, were inclined to find his
conversation arrestingly one-sided, but this will hardly serve as an
explanation of what is happening here. If the young Coleridge had
difficulty in finding an accurate description for these early poems,
it was for the good reason that nothing like them had happened
in English poetry before. Cowper, with his 'divine chit chat' (*CL*
i 279), may have taught Coleridge something about the quietly
passionate and egotistical tone in which much of these poems is
cast: but no whole Cowper poem is radically built like these,
where the poet addresses a wife, a loved one or a friend in a shifting
but shapely pattern of expostulation and private reflection. In these
poems, most characteristically, apostrophe alternates with meditation. The 'querulous egotism' to which Coleridge had half confessed in the preface of 1796 is here at last stripped of all hint of
the querulous. The egotism of these poems is in no way self-
regarding: on the contrary, it is the outgoing, solicitous concern
of the friend. It is a deeply commonplace, everyday experience
that these poems principally celebrate: not the passionate, self-
surrendering adoration of Shakespeare in the sonnets or of Tenny-

son in *In Memoriam*, but simply the deep, broad, domestic affections
of father, husband and friend that the poetry of Europe has elsewhere tended to neglect as too modest, fleeting, and undramatic a
theme.

The conversation poems also look, by hindsight, as if they were
a natural extension of Coleridge's early poetic life. His early
imitations of diverse style, beginning as a schoolboy in the 1780's
and revealing his intelligence rather than his talent, had given way
in 1794, at first manhood, to the Miltonizing 'effusions' that represented a clear talent at its undisciplined worst. A hint of unease
occurs as early as a poem of December 1794, 'To a Friend', sent to
Lamb with an unfinished version of 'Religious Musings':

> Thus far my scanty brain hath built the rhyme
> Elaborate and swelling: yet the heart
> Not owns it . . . (*CPW* 78).

In the mid-1790's, dissatisfied with 'the rhyme elaborate', Coleridge
seems suddenly to have turned towards poetic chastity. In a letter
to Southey, in the same month, he edited his friend's florid draft
of the poem 'The Pauper's Funeral' through what he called the
'compression' of an *'editio purgata'*, on the grounds that, in its
extended form, 'it wants compactness and totality—the same thought
is repeated too frequently in different words' (*CL* i 133-4). This gear-
change in Coleridge's poetic career, which broadly coincides with
the year of his greatest literary intimacy with his schoolboy friend
Charles Lamb, can be plotted in surviving letters with surprising
accuracy. Coleridge had settled in Bristol early in 1795, at the height
of his enthusiasm for Pantisocracy and its project for a new property-
less community in Pennsylvania, in order to be near Southey; and
the two poets married the Fricker sisters, who were to accompany
them to America, in the autumn of that year. By September 1795
the friendship had been breached by what appeared to Coleridge to
be Southey's lack of idealism in refusing to abandon his own claims
to property on the Susquehanna. The full intimacy of Wordsworth's
friendship hardly began until July 1797, when William and his sister
Dorothy moved to Alfoxden, near Nether Stowey in Somerset, in
order to be near their new friend. Lamb's influence shows itself

most strongly in letters of the intervening period, between May 1796 and February 1797, and it is an influence in favour of the conversation poem and, in the main, against the exclamatory language of the pantisocratic period. Lamb, in outspoken advice to the older poet on his manuscript poems, showed himself an advocate of Burns and Cowper, hostile to Milton as a model, and insistent on the virtues of simplicity and compression, of what he calls the 'energic'. 'Write thus,' he wrote boldly on receiving a copy of 'The Eolian Harp', the first conversation poem, 'and you most generally have written thus, and I shall never quarrel with you about simplicity.' It was Lamb who helped Coleridge towards healthier models: 'Burns was the god of my idolatory,' he wrote in December 1796, 'as Bowles of yours. I am jealous of your fraternising with Bowles, when I think you relish him more than Burns or my old favourite, Cowper.'[1] And yet, in spite of this plain speaking, Coleridge's movement from the effusion to the conversation poem was an evolution rather than a single leap. No great gulf is fixed between the worlds of Bowles and Cowper. Cowper, after all, is a Miltonizer too, if a more critical and sardonic disciple of Milton, and in the flux and reflux of *The Task* (1785) it is often and designedly difficult to distinguish the satirical imitations of Milton from the solemn. Bowles, it is true, is the more sentimental of the two, but then sentiment remains an indispensable aspect of the conversation poems. A good deal of the old, effusive manner lingers on in 'The Eolian Harp' and after, not always to disadvantage. The essentially sentimental notion of a place evoking a time and a set of moral reflections, which Wordsworth late in 1798 turned to such momentous effect in 'Tintern Abbey', lies at the heart of what Bowles had done in his sonnets, and it is not foreign to what Coleridge came to achieve in the conversation poems; though now the occasion of the poem is less often a mere landscape than a human tie. The stimulus now is man, but man set in a landscape which may still yield parallels of a moral kind: the just vehicle, as one can now perceive, for a poet fascinated with the status of the poem as something obscurely hovering between mind and nature, between a thought and a thing.

[1] *Letters of Charles Lamb*, ed. E. V. Lucas, London (1935), vol. i, pp. 17, 73.

Cowper fitted the new mood precisely; and Coleridge needed the example, if only to give him courage to write in a tone keyed down towards the tone of talk. This 'milder muse', as he later admiringly called Cowper, this first of modern poets, and until Wordsworth the best,[2] was the stepping-stone which helped him towards that 'daring humbleness of language and versification' (CL ii 830) which he later associated with the finest of Wordsworth. But it was the example of Cowper and the injunctions of Lamb, and not Wordsworth, that showed him the way to it. The miraculous fact of the Wordsworth friendship was that in Wordsworth he found a poet capable of executing better, above all more fully and consistently, what he was already trying to do himself: blank-verse meditations alternating between calm and passion that Coleridge himself had begun writing as early as 1795. At that date, it should be remembered, Wordsworth had scarcely written in blank verse at all, apart from the juvenile attempt at a Shakespearean tragedy in *The Borderers*; though 'The Ruined Cottage', later worked into the tissue of *The Excursion* (1814), may have been begun as early as 1795. At all events, the appearance of Coleridge's *Poems on Various Subjects* in April 1796, including 'The Eolian Harp' among other 'Effusions', establishes two facts beyond cavil: that Coleridge was already a poet of original accomplishment before he knew Wordsworth; and that he is rather more likely than Wordsworth to have evolved the blank-verse monody which he came to call the conversation poem and which, in Wordsworth's more industrious hand, became 'Tintern Abbey' and, in a vastly extended form, the *Prelude* of 1805.

Which are the conversation poems of Coleridge? The answer is bound to seem a little confused. All his life he was given to writing poems of a confessional bent; among the best of them is the 'Pains of Sleep' which he sent to Southey in a letter of September 1803 (*CL* ii 982-4)—an unusually well directed and shapely poem lamenting his frustrated love for Sara Hutchinson, and one in a mode of writing in which his facility was more often inclined to lead him into a chaos of language than into a disciplined work of any kind.

---

[2] *BL* xix, iii; Hazlitt, in 'My First Acquaintance with Poets', reporting a conversation of 1798, recalled that 'he spoke of Cowper as the best modern poet'.

But the conversation poems differ from the merely confessional in being addressed to someone, and then to a real person—or to the Somerset cottage where he spent his honeymoon, in the case of the 'Reflections on Having Left a Place of Retirement'—and their excellence derives from the shape and direction that this fact confers. There are borderline cases; and the form arises so naturally out of the earlier effusion that Coleridge may never have had much reason to think of them as a distinct category of his poetry, though there is no doubt that he designed something in the quietness of their manner, something *'sermoni propriora'*,[3] which was novel for him. The list, in fact, remains problematical. It begins with 'The Eolian Harp', dated in the *Poems* of 1796 as 'Composed August 20th, 1795, at Clevedon, Somersetshire', though its terms rather suggest that it dates from after his marriage to Sara Fricker in October 1795. The 'Harp' fully exemplifies the to-and-fro between the particular and the general that characterizes the conversation poems—from an effusive apostrophe which sets the scene:

> My pensive Sara! thy soft cheek reclined
> Thus on mine arm, most soothing sweet it is
> To sit beside our cot . . . (*CPW* 100).

with the harp 'placed length-ways in the clasping casement' for the wind to make music in; to the general reflection, provoked by its example, that the poet is part of 'the one Life within us and abroad'; and so back to a Somerset scene:

> And thus, my Love! . . .
> Full many a thought uncall'd and undetain'd,
> And many idle flitting phantasies
> Traverse my indolent and passive brain . . .

There follows a movement back to the general, in the most far-reaching reflection of all:

[3] 'Apter for prose or conversation', Horace, *Satires* I iv 42 (*'sermoni propiora'*), the motto prefixed to 'Reflections on Having left a Place of Retirement' in the *Poems* of 1797; cf *BL* i.

> And what if all of animated nature
> Be but organic harps diversely fram'd,
> That tremble into thought . . . ?

The poem seems on the point of authoritative utterance, and it is only the return of the poem to its starting-point:

> But thy more serious eye a mild reproof
> Darts, O beloved Woman! . . .

that proves the weak link in what might otherwise have been a poem that elegantly solved the early romantic dilemma of a poetry without an audience. The 'Harp' opens and closes with a captive audience of one, and its general purpose, until its unfortunate close, arises gently and effortlessly out of the domestic image of the harp in the window. But the pious figure of Sara at the end, the wife who has 'holily disprais'd These shapings of the unregenerate mind', casts a disturbing doubt on her sympathy as a listener, and fatally attracts attention to a fact otherwise hardly to be noticed at all: that the apostrophe with which the poem opens has no greater function than the humiliating necessity of finding some audience, however inapt, to release the 'aye-bubbling spring' of Philosophy. The blunt fact is that Sara is merely a nuisance in the poem, which ought to have closed on the penultimate paragraph:

> as o'er them sweeps
> Plastic and vast, one intellectual breeze,
> At once the Soul of each, and God of all.

But the 'Harp' remains a fair success in itself, and something more than a poem in which a vital formula is discovered. Indeed it asserts that formula with larger effect than the ensuing 'Reflections on Having Left a Place of Retirement', a poem written in the course of 1796 on abandoning the Somerset cottage to return to Bristol. It was to this poem, on first collecting it in the *Poems* of 1797, that Coleridge prefixed the Horatian motto *'sermoni propriora'*, and the tone represents the cool new style that he was affecting in the mid-nineties; even though the movement of the poem, which is addressed to the cottage, is less exacting and less rewarding than that of the 'Harp'. The opening account of the country seclusion abandoned out of a sense of duty strikes the new note of these poems, admitting sentiment and yet scrupulously bare of the exclamatory and the polysyllabic, and of a cool, low-pitched intensity of sentiment:

> Low was our pretty cot: our tallest rose
> Peep'd at the chamber-window. We could hear
> At silent noon, and eve, and early morn,
> The sea's faint murmur . . . (*CPW* 106).

Regret for domestic convenience is perhaps too pale a theme to take much life even from such exquisitely muted language, and Coleridge's only expedient to brace it up is a return into the old effusiveness:

> the whole world
> Seem'd imag'd in its vast circumference:
> No wish profan'd my overwhelméd heart.
> Blest hour! It was a luxury—to be!

The poem does not fail, even though it has to survive an uncertainty of manner and a self-congratulatory close: and even this close is too pregnant of possibilities, for Wordsworth as well as for Coleridge, to be without interest:

> Yet oft when after honourable toil
> Rests the tir'd mind, and waking loves to dream,
> My spirit shall revisit thee, dear cot!

This is near enough to the Wordsworth of 'Tintern Abbey', or of the host of golden daffodils, to make the reader blink.

The memory-poem, contrasting present pain or duty with past joy, with objects of past life employed as a kind of moral savings-account ('For oft, when on my couch I lie . . .') was to turn a year later into 'This Lime-Tree Bower my Prison' of June or July 1797, the first clear success among this group of poems, written at the beginning of Coleridge's *annus mirabilis* soon after settling at

Nether Stowey. It is aptly addressed to Lamb, whose critical letters
had just helped him to remake the language of his poetry, and it
realizes his reforms more perfectly than anything before it. Lamb
and the Wordsworths had left him, because of an accident to his
foot, seated in a garden, while he imagines their country walk; and
the balance of the poem lies between the simple warmth of his
friendship for them, on the one hand, and the disturbing force of
the poetic mood on the other, rising rapidly from the mild facetious-
ness of the opening to a gentle, moderated ecstasy. It is a balance
that is achieved now with an ease that only Wordsworth need not
have envied:

> Well, they are gone, and here must I remain,
> This lime-tree bower my prison! I have lost
> Beauties and feelings, such as would have been
> Most sweet to my remembrance even when age
> Had dimm'd mine eyes to blindness . . (*CPW* 178-9).

This little poem effortlessly digests within itself much of the past,
present and immediate future of English poetry. Its shape is the
familiar alternation of the conversation poem, turning from friendship to the pleasures of remembered experience and back to a friendship based on the sharing of those pleasures:

> For thee, my gentle-hearted Charles, to whom
> No sound is dissonant which tells of Life.

But it erupts into passages that predict another kind of achievement not quite born; into the world of 'Christabel' and 'Kubla
Khan', in its first paragraph, faintly eerie and fleetingly symbolic:

> The roaring dell, o'erwooded, narrow, deep,
> And only speckled by the mid-day sun;
> Where its slim trunk the ash from rock to rock
> Flings arching like a bridge;—that branchless ash
> Unsunn'd and damp, whose few poor yellow leaves
> Ne'er tremble in the gale, yet tremble still,
> Fann'd by the waterfall . . .

And, still more strikingly, there is the clear anticipation of the note of Wordsworth's 'Tintern Abbey':

> Henceforth I shall know
> That Nature ne'er deserts the wise and pure;
> No plot so narrow, be but Nature there,
> No waste so vacant, but may well employ
> Each faculty of sense, and keep the heart
> Awake to love and beauty . . .

What Wordsworth made of this a year later, in an address to his sister, is deservedly better known:

> and this prayer I make,
> Knowing that Nature never did betray
> The heart that loved her; 'tis her privilege,
> Through all the years of this our life, to lead
> From joy to joy: for she can so inform
> The mind within us . . .

The one is built weightily upon the other, and to juxtapose them in this way is to risk 'killing' Coleridge's poem outright. And it is not only Wordsworth's weight that impresses. It is his superior fertility in a mode that his friend had helped him to find. Conceptually much the less intelligent of the two, he is yet, as a poet, very much the longer-breathed. The oscillations of tone in 'Tintern Abbey' are wider, and also better controlled, than anything Coleridge was ever to achieve in the conversation poem. Even the final release of brotherly affection for Dorothy at the end of 'Tintern Abbey' exactly parallels Coleridge's summary eulogy to Lamb, but in no summary form:

> . . . Therefore let the moon
> Shine on thee in thy solitary walk,
> And let the misty mountain-winds be free
> To blow against thee . . .

This is to take possession with a giant hand. But Coleridge's grasp of his own form, if less masterful than this, is still complete.

F

And 'Frost at Midnight' of February 1798 shows how complete it was. The poem is addressed to his infant son Hartley, asleep at his side. It did not achieve its final shape until 1828, and in its first draft included a final passage of six lines scarcely less bathetic than the unfortunate close of 'The Eolian Harp'. If we attend to the ultimate draft, however, everything seems magnificently under control. The fluctuations of the poem between the poet's hopes for his son and his memories of his own childhood are now so subtle as to be scarcely numerable, like the quivering of a needle; and so much occurs that it is difficult to believe that the poem is only 74 lines long:

> For I' was reared
> In the great city, pent 'mid cloisters dim,
> And saw nought lovely but the sky and stars.
> But thou, my babe! shalt wander like a breeze
> By lakes and sandy shores . . . (*CPW* 242).

The famous 'return' of the poem upon itself, from the midnight frost, through an alternating meditation, and back to the frost which mysteriously gave rise to the meditation, is so gently effected that the reader is encouraged to notice only minor aspects of the poet's skill, such as the obtrusive relation between the opening line—

> The frost performs its secret ministry·

and the last but two—

> Or if the secret ministry of frost

while the true relation between the frost and the meditation at the heart of the poem is left a matter of faint suggestion. The verbal repetition of 'secret ministry', after all, is only the deliberately distracting gesture by which the conjuror effects his deception, for what really binds the close of the poem to its opening is the unifying reflection that even February weather is beautiful; and what binds the intermediate meditation to both is the hope that Hartley may grow to feel so too:

> Therefore all seasons shall be sweet to thee . . .

A poet who can work as well as this within such limits is capable of nearly anything. But then 'Frost at Midnight' was written in the same winter as 'The Ancient Mariner'.

'Fears in Solitude', written two months later during an invasion-scare, shows how precarious Coleridge's new achievement was. It is a shameless return to the older, effusive manner, evidently written in a white heat of patriotic indignation against the degradation of English public opinion during the French wars, and it is only by stretching charity that it can be considered a conversation poem at all. Addressed to God, if to anyone, it deprives itself by its confused political purpose of direction and of discretion too. 'The Nightingale', subtitled by Coleridge 'A Conversational Poem' and composed in the same month of April 1798, is a much more cheerful case. One of Coleridge's four contributions to the *Lyrical Ballads*, it was sub-stituted at the last moment for 'Lewti', which might have betrayed the authorship of the volume. It is always dangerous to attribute special carelessness to Coleridge: in a sense he was always a care-less, a 'facile' poet, and one in whom facility could be a virtue or a vice; but 'The Nightingale' has a scattered air, as if it had been written with an altogether exceptional indifference to design and scale. True, the conversation poem permits and even encourages the digressive; but it does move between two poles—the particular occasion and the general reflections to which that occasion gives rise—and it does return, ideally, to the friend to whom it was first addressed. 'The Nightingale' does not fulfil these unexacting stan-dards in any simple way, though it comes near, at moments, to seeming one of the most considerable of Coleridge's poems. It begins by setting the scene—a cloudless sunset, a bridge, and a nightingale —with that particularity of utterance that Coleridge had imported into this group of poems from the language of the late Augustans and which he was to use to ironic effect, perhaps in the following month, in the opening paragraph of 'Kubla Khan':

> No cloud, no relique of the sunken day
> Distinguishes the West, no long thin slip
> Of sullen light, no obscure trembling hues . . . (*CPW* 264).

The manner lifts itself, not quite without a hint of the laborious,

and then oddly thrusts solemnity aside with an overt quotation
from Milton's 'Il Penseroso':

> And hark! the nightingale begins its song,
> 'Most musical, most melancholy' bird.
> A melancholy bird? . . .

This is strange usage of an elder poet, and seemingly disruptive,
but the rejection of Milton justifies itself as the poem proceeds. The
point, as it emerges in the second paragraph, is the familiar one
of the joyousness of all natural objects. Bursting, at last, into an
address to William and Dorothy Wordsworth, ('My Friend, and
thou, our Sister') the poet calls on their support against Milton
and the Miltonizers:

> we have learnt
> A different lore: we may not thus profane
> Nature's sweet voices, always full of love
> And joyance!

In Nature, in spite of Milton, 'there is nothing melancholy', though
'many a poet echoes the conceit' of the nightingale's sad song. The
whole skirmish suggests how unevenly the language of these poems
coexists with the Miltonics of late eighteenth-century blank verse.
It is itself Miltonic in an infinity of ways—in the abundance of
enjambement, in the inversions and suspensions of syntax—while
the word 'joyance', which Coleridge seems to have re-introduced
into English poetry, is from Spenser.[4] But the relationship is alter-
nately one of attraction and repulsion, an alternation of miltonizing
and anti-miltonizing. It is an alternation that might well have
succeeded if only the poem had not wandered off in its last
two stanzas to describe 'a most gentle maid' who has loved the
nightingales, and to tell a sentimental 'father's tale' of the infant

---

[4] *Faerie Queene* III xii 18. Coleridge had already used the word five years before,
in 'Lines on an Autumnal Evening', l. 16 (*CPW* 51), and was to use it again in a
late addition to 'The Eolian Harp' (*CPW* 101). Shelley borrowed it twenty-two
years after *Lyrical Ballads* in 'To a Skylark'. l. 76:
> With thy clear keen joyance
> Languor cannot be.

Hartley's reaction to their song. The final address to William and Dorothy ('one more, my friends! farewell') is too perfunctory to pull the poem back into shape. As it is, it quivers into life, and unexpectedly, in the third paragraph, where a memory of the nightingale is evoked in bright, nervous little flashes of words— a language Coleridge cannot have learned from anyone, and which he bequeathed to Shelley and Keats:

> On moonlight bushes,
> Whose dewy leaflets are but half-disclosed,
> You may perchance behold them on the twigs,
> Their bright, bright eyes, their eyes both bright and full,
> Glistening, while many a glow-worm in the shade
> Lights up her love-torch.

This is the most surprising Coleridge of all, the Coleridge who seemed to his contemporaries the purest of poets because the least substantial, and the best able to make a poem out of nothing but words. Pater was to call it 'his rich delicate dreaminess'. Glycine's song in *Zapolya*, years later, arrests by surprising in the same way, and a comparison with Tieck's 'Herbstlied', which it adapts, would only show how little Coleridge owes to the German:

> He sank, he rose, he twinkled, he trolled
>     Within that shaft of sunny mist;
> His eyes of fire, his beak of gold,
>     All else of amethyst (*CPW* 919).

The most extended of the conversation poems is the Dejection Ode—or more precisely, the first version of the ode which he sent to Sara Hutchinson, whom he had loved hopelessly for more than two years, in a letter of 4 April 1802 (*CL* ii 790-8).[5] It demands some justification to call it a conversation poem at all. It is, of course, a Pindaric Ode, like the Immortality Ode that Wordsworth had

---

[5] The autograph manuscript of the first and longest version of the poem, now at Dove Cottage, Grasmere, was first edited by Ernest de Selincourt in *Essays and Studies* xxii (1937). The best text is in George Whalley, *Coleridge and Sara Hutchinson and the Asra Poems*, London (1955), pp. 155-64.

begun writing a few days before, and both poems reveal the irregular rhyme pattern and the interspersing of long and short lines which the neoclassical age, not very accurately, had associated with Pindar, whereas the characteristic metre of the conversation poem is blank verse. And yet 'Dejection' is much more like 'Frost at Midnight', in everything but metre, than it is like Coleridge's previous attempts at the ode. Especially in its first and longest form, as a poetical letter of 340 lines, it is a very private poem. And many private elements uncomfortably survive even when shortened into its first published form, in the *Morning Post* of October 1802, where the noncommittal 'Edmund' is substituted for the 'Sara' of the first version, and the 'Wordsworth' of another (*CL* ii 815-9); or in the ultimate form of *Sibylline Leaves* (1817), where the matter of sex is finally righted with the formal apostrophe 'Lady!'. The reader depends on editors, for example, to explain that in the last stanza but one the 'tale of less affright' of 'a little child Upon a lonesome wild' refers to Wordsworth's 'Lucy Gray', which had appeared in the second edition of *Lyrical Ballads* in 1800; and the odd relation that 'Dejection' bears to the Immortality Ode is one that only an intimate member of the Wordsworth circle could understand without a gloss. It seems best to think of the first version of 1802 as a conversation poem which, by some vagary, has been cast into the form of a rough-and-ready ode. In the ensuing months it was trimmed to less than half its original length, purged of most of its private reference, and set forth upon the world as one of the oddest compromises in English poetry: an intensely, bitterly, almost indecently private poem of an unhappily married poet, cast into that most public of all forms, the neoclassical Pindaric. The language swirls upwards and downwards from a studiously conversational opening ('Well! If the Bard was weather-wise . . .') to passages of a grave sublimity that Coleridge had scarcely ever achieved. Not since 'The Ancient Mariner' of four years before had his doctrine of deliberately incongruous form realized anything so arresting. It is by this startling contrast of the formal and the informal that the poem lives, and for just this reason there can be no doubt of the superiority of the final version, where the original 340 lines have been reduced to a tight-packed 139. Coleridge is so exuberant a poet, and so little self-critical in his creative moments, that it is exceptional to watch him at work, as here, with the pruning-hook. Of course he had private and prudential reasons for cutting— reasons which had nothing to do with poetic merit. But, as it happily falls out, the most private passages in the original Letter are also, on the whole, the most dispensable. Coleridge is often at his worst when most sincere. No one could regret the loss of

> I read thy guileless letter o'er again—
> I hear thee of thy blameless self complain—
> And only this I learn—and this, alas! I know—
> That thou art weak and pale with sickness, grief and pain—
> And I—*I* made thee so!

Perhaps the only passage in the Letter to be regretted is the moment when even that feverish and frustrated love breaks into something monumentally grave:

> Be happy, and I need thee not in sight.
> Peace in thy heart, and quiet in thy dwelling,
> Health in thy limbs, and in thine eyes the light
> Of love, and hope, and honourable feeling . . .

On the whole, it is surely clear, the reduction of the ode to its familiar form is a continuous triumph of critical acumen.

The Dejection Ode, too, represents the height of Coleridge's poetic intimacy with Wordsworth since the *Lyrical Ballads* of four years before. That intimacy, in many ways and avowedly, was from the start a meeting of opposite temperaments, and it was to prove so various in its poetic effects that it is difficult even at this distance to sum it up. Wordsworth's mature poetic language—the language, say, of 'Tintern Abbey' or of the 1805 *Prelude*—was not one of Coleridge's 'assumptions', something he could travesty or put on like an old garment. It was in some measure his own invention; it was something that belonged to him as much as it belonged to Wordsworth. When, in 1797, the two young poets divided the world of poetry between the supernatural and the everyday (*BL* xiv), there is no reason to suppose that they thought the division directly represented the nature of their individual talents, though it may in some sense have represented their current inclinations. Coleridge, after all, had been writing conversation poems about the everyday for two years, and Wordsworth was to collaborate actively in the composition of 'The Ancient Mariner' and may have written an early draft of 'Lewti'. Once, at least, they indulged themselves in a composition-race to write different parts of the same work, a race that ended in Coleridge's prose fragment 'The Wanderings of Cain'. And yet there are ranges and depths in each poet which, one ultimately feels, were forever inaccessible to the other. The tragic bitterness which Coleridge reveals in his talent for the night-marish, as in the central stanzas of 'The Ancient Mariner', make Wordsworth seem almost an emotional prig; and, at the same time, Coleridge seems never to have been patient enough to achieve in verse those long, emotional explorations of feeling, those minute diagrams of human perception at which Wordsworth excelled. The proximity of Wordsworth's Immortality Ode and Coleridge's Dejection emphasize both the sympathy and the contrast: the vast areas in which the two men were at one, the recesses of mind where each remained private and alone. Coleridge had already written 'The Mad Monk', a dramatic monologue put in the mouth of a crazed Sicilian which had appeared in the *Morning Post* (13 October 1800). It contained the lines:

> There was a time when earth, and sea, and skies,
>   The bright green vale, and forest's dark recess,
> With all things, lay before mine eyes
>   In steady loveliness:
> But now . . . (*CPW* 348).

Wordsworth began the first ode he ever wrote on 27th March 1802, according to Dorothy's journal, and in terms which gratefully accepted more than a version of the metre from Coleridge:

> There was a time when meadow, grove and stream,
>   The earth, and every common sight,
>     To me did seem
>   Apparelled in celestial light,

> The glory and the freshness of a dream.
> It is not now as it hath been of yore . . .

The first four stanzas, which are all he wrote on that March morning, are among the oddest turns of his genius. To borrow from a friend was normal enough; but to borrow in the form of an ode, something that must then have seemed peculiarly the property of Coleridge, and then to turn the ode back to its Renaissance sources in phrases like 'apparelled in celestial light', all suggests an antiquarian choice of unexpected sophistication. In the event, as he finished the poem, perhaps early in 1804, he made of it the most convincing re-creation that we have in the last two hundred years of the festive world of Spenser's 'Epithalamion' or of Milton's Nativity Ode—

> And while the young lambs bound
> As to the tabor's sound—

and a striking illustration of the romantic principle of incongruity, since the poem remains a personal statement, in full defiance of its assumption of the form and manner of a public poem.

The rest of the story is better known. William and Dorothy left for Keswick on the next day of March 1802 to be with Coleridge. A few days later, between sunset and midnight, and while the Wordsworths were still there, Coleridge wrote the long verse letter to Sara Hutchinson that forms the first version of the poem, echoing in his own outpouring two lines from Wordsworth's fragment (Immortality Ode, ll.9 and 40), notably the Spenserian word 'coronal'. If it is assumed, as it is natural to assume, that the first four stanzas of the Immortality Ode were the poetic stimulus for this burst of creativity, certain problems relating to the first Dejection Ode become easier to solve. It is a self-contradictory thing—a personal, even self-revelatory, ode; but then Wordsworth had just shown him that blank verse is not the only metre proper for such poems, and had shown him by using a passage from his own 'Mad Monk'. And, like the Immortality Ode, the Dejection turns back upon itself to re-assert the public function of the ode by making a case of general as well as of private concern. Parts of Coleridge's ode

even read like an answer to the question posed by Wordsworth at
the point where his unfinished poem, in the spring of 1802, had
come to rest:

> Whither is fled the visionary gleam?
> Where is it now, the glory and the dream?

The two poems are in some sense in a dialogue with each other.
As it happens, the very question, and the answer Wordsworth was
later to supply, are both in outline familiar in his poetry. Something like them both occur in 'Tintern Abbey', written nearly four
years before. The cost of manhood, and the 'abundant recompense'
which the intellectual life offers in exchange for the life of the
instincts, was already a familiar concern to him, and his mind was
currently engaged upon it elsewhere, in the *Prelude*. There is no
reason to suppose, in fact, that Wordsworth needed Coleridge to
finish his poem. But each poet seems to have needed the other to
start. Wordsworth had evidently turned to an earlier Coleridge
poem to solve a problem of form; Coleridge now used an unfinished
poem of Wordsworth's to solve a problem of conscience. Both
poems, as we finally possess them, reconcile the private and the
public in a manner characteristic of the conversation poem, and
both exploit the status of the ode to do something else as well: to
dignify a private reflection into a formal theology of the religion
of Nature, the doctrine by which natural objects and events may
be used to evoke a reality within. The world must prove impotent,
of course, when nothing is left within us to evoke. Coleridge's
statement is characteristically the blunter and rawer of the two:

> O Lady! we receive but what we give,
> And in our life alone does Nature live:
> Ours is her wedding garment, ours her shroud!
>   And would we aught behold, of higher worth
> Than that inanimate cold world allowed
> To the poor loveless ever-anxious crowd,
>   Ah! from the soul itself must issue forth
> A light, a glory, a fair luminous cloud
>   Enveloping the earth . . .

This expostulatory tone is quite unlike anything in Wordsworth's poem, and for once even the points of exclamation are hardly to be resented. This truth, unlike Wordsworth's, is genuinely a bitter truth. In exchange for Wordsworth's 'abundant recompense' Coleridge offers nothing at all, and the loss of the 'shaping spirit' conferred at birth is rewarded only by the tedious nightmare of a life of pure intellect, all the more agonizing because self-inflicted:

> For not to think of what I needs must feel,
>   But to be still and patient, all I can;
> And haply by abstruse research to steal
> From my own nature all the natural man—
> This was my sole resource, my only plan . . .

In the final version, from which I quote here, the problem of conscience is tactfully obscured: Coleridge's unrequited love for Sara Hutchinson, to whom the poem is addressed, had itself been a model for the suppression of 'the natural man'. And yet the problem is not lost. In the earlier conversation poems the parodoxical contrast between the minor, domestic occasion and the mighty reflections to which the occasion might give rise had seemed a matter for congratulation, and it remains so in Wordsworth's conclusion to the Immortality Ode:

> To me the meanest flower that blows can give
> Thoughts that do often lie too deep for tears.

In the Dejection Ode the same familiar paradox is a paradox of horror. The language of cool particularity which Coleridge had developed in the earlier poems is now used, with brutal precision, to evoke a mood of Life-in-Death frigidity:

> . . . Have I been gazing on the western sky
> And its peculiar tint of yellow green:
> And still I gaze—and with how blank an eye! . . .
> I see them all so excellently fair,
> I see, not feel, how beautiful they are!

The Dejection Ode, even in its final form, may seem to fall just short of masterly utterance, and clearly short of the Immortality Ode to which, in some fashion, it owes its existence; perhaps because the gentle alternations between the cosmic and the particular seem too loose and too informal for matter as grave, even as grim, as this. The shaping spirit has here been content not to shape, but merely to prune. And only a profound sense of poetic formality could have pointed the desired contrast and made a work of art of so private a grief. In the Dejection Ode Coleridge abandoned too little of the conversation poem, perhaps, when he abandoned only its characteristic metre. He pushed it insistently towards a point to which, in its nature, it could hardly attain.

The verse-letter of January 1808 'To William Wordsworth', composed (according to its subtitle in *Sibylline Leaves*) 'on the Night after his Recitation of a Poem on the Growth of an Individual Mind', returns to the familiar dress of blank verse and suffers from no such strain. It is the last pure example that Coleridge's poetry affords of the conversation poem, being written immediately after his return from two years of work and wandering in Malta and Italy (1804-6); and the surviving manuscripts of the poem show how, after its first rapid composition on the night that Wordsworth read him the *Prelude* at Coleorton, it was trimmed to its published form. In such a poem of loving friendship and self-abasement, little could usefully be done to render the poem public enough for *Sibylline Leaves* (1817), where it first appeared, and on this occasion the hand of self-censorship moved less surely than it had done over the manuscript of the Dejection Ode. But then the poem is extravagant in its very being. It celebrates the greatest friendship in our literary history as well as the greatest autobiography in verse, and that an autobiography which was itself addressed to Coleridge and offered as a tribute to his genius. Even at this great distance the situation seems more painful than could be wished. Coleridge's praise for the *Prelude* is limitless; and yet, after the alternating fashion of the conversation poem, it is intermixed with reflective moods in which he allows himself to recall his own relative lack of achievement. The generosity of such a tribute, its startling freedom from envy, would even in a better poem have been hard to bear. As it is, the poem descends into self-embarrassment to a point where, more than once, the poet has to call himself to order, from the contemplation of his own empty and wandering life to the spectacle of a realized poem:

> That way no more! and ill beseems it me,
> Who came a welcomer in herald's guise,
> Singing of glory, and futurity,
> To wander back on such unhealthful road,
> Plucking the poisons of self-harm! And ill
> Such intertwine beseems triumphal wreaths
> Strew'd before thy advancing! (CPW 407).

It is an emotional embarrassment the reader can do little but share. 'Unhealthful' is just what it is, and though great poetry may be made of unhealthy emotions, such a clear awareness of the morbid, in so knowing a poet, is certain to prove self-inhibiting. And yet the poem remains clearly considerable. Its second paragraph, which is the first critique of the *Prelude* that we have, shows how inwardly Coleridge knew what that poem was about:

> . . . Of tides obedient to external force,
> And currents self-determined, as might seem,
> Or by some inner power; of moments awful,
> Now in thy inner life, and now abroad,
> When power streamed from thee, and thy soul received
> The light reflected as a light bestowed . . .

The interplay of external and internal, which is the life of the conversation poem, is the life of the *Prelude* too, and the language of Wordsworth's poem is seen here as mysteriously involved in the exchange between the world without and the world within:

> An Orphic song indeed,
> A song divine of high and passionate thoughts
> To their own music chaunted.

This mystery of language is evidenced in 'To William Wordsworth' itself, and no wonder, since Coleridge insists at the close upon the hypnotic power of what he has heard:

And when—O Friend! my comforter and guide!
Strong in thyself, and powerful to give strength!
Thy long sustainéd Song finally closed,
And thy deep voice had ceased—yet thou thyself
Wert still before my eyes, and round us both
That happy vision of belovéd faces—
Scarce conscious, and yet conscious of its close
I sate, my being blended in one thought
(Thought was it? or aspiration? or resolve?)
Absorbed, yet hanging still upon the sound—
And when I rose, I found myself in prayer.

In such a conclusion the reader may readily forget the clumsy Miltonism of the opening paragraph and the dizzying emotional abysses at the core of the poem. This, after all, is the language of the *Prelude* itself that he now hears, an imitation executed under such passionate pressure, and out of so deep an intimacy with a language that Coleridge had, after all, helped to make, that it imposes itself without presumption as the original itself.

It is tempting to say that here, and only here, in the conversation poems, Coleridge spoke with his own voice and without 'assumption' of style. But Coleridge is the last poet to let us say so. All his poetic life he knew that the language of poetry must in some sense hold itself aloof. If the conversation poems seem unassuming, it is surely not because they are genuinely like conversation, but rather because the styles they imitate are so numerous and so richly intermixed: not only Miltonisms and anti-Miltonisms, but the effusive tone of Gray as well as the plainness of Cowper. The impression of naturalism is created not so much by genuinely colloquial language as by the kaleidoscopic movement from style to style. At times, it is true, they seem otherwise, and leave an impression of being uniquely authentic, as if one were 'listening to Coleridge talking; not to a poetic statement, but to a section cut from a stream of talk';[6] but this can only be an illusion. The illusion is perhaps fully significant, the diction designed to deceive in just this way; but the formality of these poems emerges, after close observation, as a fact to be observed. They solve in a pro-

[6] Donald Davie, *Purity of Diction in English Verse*, London (1952), p. 124.

82

visional way the cardinal difficulty of the first romantic poets—
the difficulty that (as Samuel Butler once bluntly put it) language
needs a sayee as well as a sayer—and they solve it by addressing
the poem to a member of a closed circle of family and friends. This
might in itself have proved a trivial achievement, ending in nothing but a series of verse epistles of a familiar Augustan kind. In
fact these poems, at their best, seem to be shapely in a new sense,
and the shape which they achieved as early as the mid-1790's represents a bold advance towards a novel kind of poetry. Europe
has since learned to call that kind symbolic. The famous 'return'
of the conversation poem to the starting-point, most perfectly
realized in 'Frost at Midnight', later confers shape upon some of
the most achieved of romantic poems, including 'Tintern Abbey'
and 'The Ancient Mariner'. The movement of such poems is a
familiar fact of experience; it is a little like that of a man who,
circling an object, is himself changed by what he sees there, so
that by the end of his journey he seems to know both the place
and himself for the first time. 'Is this mine own countree?', as the
Ancient Mariner puts it as he sails into the home port. The simple
object, such as midnight frost, or the Wye Valley, or 'the meanest
flower that blows', acts as a measuring-rod to the poet's perception
and to his 'moral being'. As a symbol, it possesses the direct advantage that, unlike his moral being, it bears to be looked at. Where
the depths are as deep as Coleridge's were, this is no mere evasion
but a matter of something like plain necessity; and even if it were
not so, the romantic symbol would remain a device of supreme
convenience as a point of entry into the fretful task of writing a
poem. It launches the poet easily upon his journey: it allows him
to start when nothing is so difficult as to start. Coleridge was aware
of the profundity of the problems raised by the poetic revolution
in which the poet's heart, rather than his social relations, became
the prime subject of poetry. He solved it by going round:

> My eloquence was most commonly excited by the desire of running
> away and hiding myself from my personal and inward feelings,
> and not for the expression of them, while doubtless this very effort
> of feeling gave a passion and glow to my thoughts and language on

subjects of a general nature, that they otherwise would not have had. I fled in a circle, still overtaken by the feelings from which I was ever more fleeing, with my back turned towards them.[7]

He knew, too, that the harder we look at the object, the more symbolic, the less itself, it may become. The cool, steady contemplation of the opening lines of the conversation poems had already exemplified the principle. Quoting from 'Tintern Abbey' in a note written early in 1801,

> . . . and the deep power of Joy,
> We see into the Life of things,

he added:

> i.e. by deep feeling we make our ideas dim—and this is what we mean by our life—ourselves. I think of the wall—it is before me, a distinct image, here . . . Now let me think of myself, of the thinking being—the idea becomes dim, whatever it be,—so dim that I know not what it is; but the feeling is deep and steady, and this I call 'I', identifying the percipient and the perceived (CN 921).

Vagueness, dimness, is an essential element in the romantic symbol, and no mere acceptance of defeat. For the new kind of analogy it offers is not simple and finite but open-ended, offering the interpreter tempting choices and additional possibilities. If we respect it, it is because, lacking precision as it does, it offers multifarious answers to a question which is itself multifarious. Precision can be inaccurate, after all. The questions posed by Coleridge in the conversation poems, which concern the whole of man's relation to the world around him, were best served by this most tentative of poetic forms.

[7] Thomas Allsop, *Letters, Conversations and Recollections of Coleridge*, London (1836), vol. ii, pp. 136-7, from a letter of 29 June 1822.

# CHAPTER SIX

# The Ancient Mariner

The conversation poems of 1795 and after bring Coleridge to the verge of symbolism: with 'The Ancient Mariner', 'Christabel' and 'Kubla Khan', all poems of 1797-1800, he plunges deeply in. Apart from Blake's *Songs of Innocence and Experience* (1789-93)—and it seems likely that Coleridge did not read Blake until as late as 1818 (*CL* iv 836-7)—no English poet had ever attempted anything like it. And yet if it is asked how, if at all, this revolution related to Coleridge's first years as an imitative poet, one is obliged to be content with an answer that falls well short of finality. The efficient cause is not to be found. One alleged cause, the friendship with Wordsworth, can be dismissed on the evidence of the dates alone: it is clear that in the early conversation poems Coleridge was already at the point of discovery before his intimacy with Wordsworth began. In the following chapters I shall try to show, but without any pretence to showing any sort of inevitability, how his three greatest poems achieve symbolism through imitative forms: the 'Mariner' through an imitation of the medieval ballad, 'Christabel' of Gothic horror, and 'Kubla Khan' of two contrasting poetic styles. And yet if there was no clear reason why the imitative had to lead to the symbolic, it is still worth observing that the two functions are beautifully compatible. The essential obliquity of poetic imitation, where all statement tends to be indirect and open to more interpretations than one, being filtered through the language of other forms and other ages, offers conditions in which symbolism is ripe to be born.

'The Ancient Mariner' represents this double vision more plainly than any other. No poem is more central to the achievement of an English poet than this poem is to Coleridge's. Not only is it the longest of his poems, and complete in every sense: it is also the most fully realized product of the pact he made with Wordsworth soon after William and Dorothy had settled near him at Alfoxden in July 1797; and though Wordsworth did not make him a great poet, it still seems likely that he dramatically influenced the kind of greatness Coleridge was to achieve. This is how, nearly twenty years later, Coleridge was to describe the pact of 1797:

> The thought suggested itself (to which of us I do not recollect) that a series of poems might be composed of two sorts. In the one [Coleridge's], the incidents and agents were to be, in part at least, supernatural . . . For the second class [Wordsworth's,] subjects were to be chosen from ordinary life . . . (*BL* xiv).

This agreement was the turning-point of Coleridge's life as a poet, since the unfinished 'Christabel' and the so-called 'fragment' 'Kubla Khan', as well as the 'Ancient Mariner' itself—a large part of Coleridge's major achievement as a poet—all issue clearly out of it. As it happened, the first edition of *Lyrical Ballads* appeared in September 1798 with only three poems by Coleridge, apart from the 'Mariner'. But the 'Mariner'—incongruous as it must have looked to the uninstructed reader of 1798—still heads an anonymous collection which Coleridge, in a letter to his publisher in May 1798, insisted was to be one work, and it offers itself as the thing that sets the tone and defines the substance of the whole, 'one work, in kind though not in degree, as an Ode is one work' (*CL* i 412). Whatever a 'lyrical ballad' is—and the term must cover a wide area if it includes the 'Ancient Mariner', 'The Idiot Boy' and 'Tintern Abbey' —the conclusion is hardly avoidable that the 'Mariner' is basic to the concept that two young poets shared, and shared out between them, during the autumn of 1797. Coleridge began work on the 'Ancient Mariner' in November 1797, a few months after Wordsworth became his neighbour, worked on it concentratedly through the Somerset winter, and brought it to Alfoxden, so Dorothy tells us in her journal, in March 1798. No other poem he wrote can have cost him so much, or have been so much worth the cost.

But more is known about the circumstances of composition than this. The two poets did not only divide the project of the

*Lyrical Ballads* between them—they also indulged themselves in a composition-race, on the set subject of Cain. 'The title and subject,' so Coleridge wrote years later, in a note to his prose poem 'The Wanderings of Cain',

> were suggested by myself, who likewise drew out the scheme and contents for each of the three books or cantos . . . My partner undertook the first canto; I the second: and which ever had done first, was to set about the third.

But Wordsworth, next morning, admitted he had done nothing, and

> the whole scheme . . . broke up in a laugh: and the 'Ancient Mariner' was written instead (*CPW* 286-7).

On late evidence, then, but the poet's own, it appears that the 'Mariner' was composed as Coleridge's supernatural counterpart to Wordsworth's poems about the domestic and the commonplace, and 'instead' of a biblical poem of sin and punishment.

This is what Coleridge tells: what appears, on examining the formal properties of the 'Ancient Mariner', is a highly literary ballad, and the most finished imitation, though by no means the first, of Percy's *Reliques* (1765). In fact it is almost the only poem in the first edition of *Lyrical Ballads* which is a ballad in this precise, historical sense, and almost the only one using the 'ballad metre' that Percy's collection had made familiar to educated readers since 1765—alternating four- and three-foot lines riming ABCB, or sometimes, with an addition of two lines, ABCBDB[1]—though there are few references to Percy in Coleridge's early notes and letters, and little concerning the form of the medieval ballad that he could not have learned from contemporary imitations such as Walter Scott's *The Chase, and William and Helen* (1796) The literary imitation of the medieval ballad is, of course, in no sense Coleridge's invention. Apart from Scott, Bürger's *Lenore* (1775) had by 1797 been translated into English over and over again (*CN* 1,132 n), and the choice of this form for a literary purpose is one of the least original decisions Coleridge ever took. Wordsworth's 'ballads', by contrast,

---

[1] Only two of Wordsworth's contributions to *1798*—'We are Seven' and 'The Tables Turned'—are strictly in ballad metre, both with a rhyming third-line (ABAB).

are mainly imitations of popular, broadsheet ballads of the eighteenth century: they are not in their form 'period', like Coleridge's poem, but vulgar—hence Wordsworth's nervous excuses in his Advertisement that the poems are mainly experiments. In spite of this claim, or apology, there are certainly formal precedents in Hannah More, Scott and elsewhere for what both poets are doing. The originality of the enterprise lies in the conjunction of the popular and the literary, a conjunction that seeks its justification as early as the title-page in the ambiguity of the term 'ballad'. 'Lyrical' means 'relating to human sentiment or emotion'—a possible but far from characteristic property of any sort of ballad in the late eighteenth century. The sharp contrast between the popular and the literary is fully asserted in the poems, in the sense that there are no border-lines cases: Wordsworth, in his ballads, defies a class prejudice, Coleridge in the 'Mariner' makes a large historical allusion of a highly literary kind. For the 'Mariner' is, among other things, an exercise in pastiche, being 'professedly written in imitation of the *style* as well as of the spirit of the elder poets', as the Advertisement of 1798 has it; and it is of the nature of this imitation, which is an unusually obscure and complex one, that it guards the inner secret of the poem. All the more obscure and complex because, in the twenty years (1797-1817) that elapsed between the first composition and the publication of the last radical revision of the poem in *Sibylline Leaves*, Coleridge altered the details of his imitation at least twice, and deliberately complicated the poem by turning a single pastiche into a double one.

There are three principal texts of the 'Ancient Mariner', representing the original poem and its two main revisions. In the first edition of *Lyrical Ballads*, or *1798*, the poem appeared at the head of the collection, in mock-medieval spelling ('The Rime of the Ancyent Marinere') and headed by a brief prose argument in modern English. For the second edition, or *1800*, perhaps feeling he had carried the joke too far, Coleridge modernized the spelling of the entire poem as well as the choice of some thirty or forty words, deleting forty-six lines and adding seven. It is in this second version, degraded by Wordsworth from its pride of place at the head of *1798* and placed almost at the end of the first volume of

88

1800, that the imitative element is at its weakest. In meeting the objections of obscurity and philological ineptitude brought by some reviewers of *1798*, if that was his motive, Coleridge risked the fate of being taken literally.

The third version of the poem, which appeared in *Sibylline Leaves* (1817), restored a sense of pastiche without resorting, as in *1798*, to medieval usages. Coleridge's solution to the problem remains to this day puzzling and idiosyncratic: he chose, apart from the addition of eighteen new lines and the deletion of nine, to leave the text of the poem essentially unchanged; but he added an 800-word prose gloss to the margin in seventeenth-century neo-Platonic prose. Since 1817, then, the imitation has been designedly complicated, since the poem still pretends to be medieval, while the gloss pretends to belong to a date between the poem and the poet. In terms of its historical element, the poem may conveniently be considered first.

'The Ancient Mariner' is packed with explicit historical information. The ballad form is associated most naturally with the fifteenth and early sixteenth centuries, when many English and Scottish ballads were thought to have been first composed or first written down; and the 'Mariner' pretends to describe, in late medieval language, a voyage taken by an English ship soon after Columbus's voyage of 1492. After Columbus, since there is no suggestion of anything very unusual or pioneering about the spirit in which the ship sets out; but before Magellan, who in 1522 was the first European to enter the Pacific by water, around the tip of South America —'we were the first that ever burst Into that silent sea' (ll. 105-6). The object of the voyage is never told. But it is broadly Magellan's route that the ship first follows, willy-nilly, and the reader is certainly meant to follow it literally, at least in Part I:

> The Sun came up upon the left,
> Out of the sea came he!
> And he shone bright, and on the right
> Went down into the sea  (*CPW* 187).

For anyone still uncertain of his bearings, the direction is plainly stated a few stanzas after:

> He struck with his o'ertaking wings
> And chased us south along . . .

> The ship drove fast, loud roared the blast,
> And southward aye we fled.

The route, then, is due south through the Atlantic, across the 'Line' (as the Gloss calls it) and terrifyingly near to the South Pole, where the albatross joins the ship and brings the ice-bound helmsman good luck and a wind to drive them northwards; and then, in Part II, after the senseless shooting of the bird, north into the Pacific till the ship again reaches the Equator and is hideously becalmed in tropical seas; until, in Part V, the Polar Spirit (but by now Coleridge's interest in the geography of his voyage is less intent and less clear) pushes the ship 'as far as the Line'—either it has drifted away, or it is now back in the Atlantic—and the dead shipmates, by what route we are left to guess, steer the ship back to its home port. The events, of course, are fantastic and 'praeternatural'. But the route itself is fantastic in the age of the ballads only to the extent that the ship is an English one. No Englishman made a journey into the Pacific Ocean until Sir Francis Drake in 1579, and he was not 'the first'. There is still enough historical evidence to date the imaginary voyage, very broadly, around 1500, a natural date for a late-medieval ballad, and consistent with the elaborately Catholic and medieval detail: the 'merry minstrelsy' of the wedding, the mariolatry of the Mariner's own language ('Heaven's mother send us grace', 'To Mary queen the praise be given'), and the Catholic assumptions of all the explicit morality of the poem, which is full of talk of shriving and penance, and includes the figure of a medieval ascetic, the Hermit, in Part VII. Some have even talked as if the Mariner himself were a medieval minstrel, but there seems to be no evidence for this: in the final version of the poem he appears to the Wedding-Guest simply as a stranger and a nuisance:

> 'Hold off! unhand me, grey-beard loon',

and in the first version of 1798 the Wedding Guest thinks he is about to tell him a funny story of the sort sailors are supposed to tell at weddings:

> 'Nay, if thou'st got a laughsome tale,
> Marinere! come with me.'

In any case, the Mariner is not like a professional story-teller. His manner is passionate, personal and obsessed, not professional—so much so that he has even, irrelevantly, been identified with the Wandering Jew: 'There was a ship . . .'; and the hypnosis he exercises over his victims, admittedly a useful gift in a professional story-teller, is clearly not a professional trick. As a matter of fact, it is revealed at the end of the poem that he feels compelled to tell the story to passers-by whenever the 'agony returns'. It is part of his penance, and apparently a kind of therapy too:

> And till my ghastly tale is told,
> This heart within me burns.

All this conforms neatly with the bargain Coleridge had struck with Wordsworth in 1797, as he later described it. Sceptical of the reality of the supernatural, he was yet deeply impressed by the reality of the emotions of those who, like the Mariner, believe themselves to have suffered such visitations. 'Real in this [dramatic] sense they have been to every human being who, from whatever source of delusion, has at any time believed himself under supernatural agency' (*BL* xiv), and no poem Coleridge ever wrote fulfils this aspect of the bargain with such exactitude.

The prose gloss, which Coleridge may have written at almost any time between 1800 and 1817, can hardly be said to add significantly to our knowledge of the action of the poem. Its interest plainly lies in the fact that it both enforces and complicates the historical allusion. Its language is richly, even extravagantly, Jacobean-Caroline, and it gives Coleridge an opportunity to display his esoteric reading in Renaissance neo-Platonism which he had begun before 1797. That it is, in the broadest sense, pastiche, is perfectly clear; and it is even possible that the longest gloss of all may be an echo of a passage in Jeremy Taylor (*CN* 1,473 n). But is it, as a whole, a pastiche of anything in particular? Not of Percy's *Reliques*, certainly, since they are not marginally glossed at all, such annotation as they have being severely explanatory and not in the least quaint; or of Ritson, who in his editions of ballads in the 1780's and 1790's merely uses scholarly end-notes. Indeed no edition of English ballads I know of is marginally glossed. And if it is asked what single seventeenth-century book Coleridge might have had in mind, there is still no certain answer to offer. Chapman's Homer (1598-1611), which Coleridge admired, especially the Odyssey (*CL* iii 67), is a verse narrative with a prose gloss by the translator himself, but the gloss is in no way quaint or neo-Platonic: it consists, usefully enough, of headings to incidents and dialogues, and excuses for his interpretations of the Greek intermixed with abuse of the Homeric commentators. Henry More and Ralph Cudworth, the Cambridge Platonists, like Purchas in his *Pilgrimage* (1613), occasionally use a gloss to identify a reference or to summarize an argument, but this is not an example of the prose glossing of verse, or of any sort of narrative; and Coleridge's favourite, Jeremy Taylor, who seems the likeliest source for Coleridge's stylistic 'assumption' here, does not employ marginal glosses at all. The fact seems to be that there is no precedent for what Coleridge is doing—a useful, if negative, conclusion. For if Coleridge's gloss is not a pastiche of any known work, it seems fair to dismiss the possibility that the relation between the gloss and the poem is meant to be recognized as a familiar one. Is it not of the essence of pastiche that it should be directed against something celebrated, a piece of public property? If the joke here depends upon recognizing a particular target among seventeenth-century authors, such as Jeremy Taylor, then it is a hopelessly private one. Nobody in a century and a half has succeeded in seeing the point of it.

What, then, is the gloss for? Some have supposed that Coleridge added it after 1800 because the early reviewers of *1798* had found the poem obscure—'a Dutch attempt at German sublimity', as Southey had rudely called it in the *Critical Review* (October 1798). But this too must be mistaken. The modernization of spelling in *1800* had already met the objection of obscurity. In any case, the gloss does not clarify: it rather complicates. A few geographical details are added, it is true, as when the Pacific and the Equator ('the Line') are specified, but any attentive reader could have guessed these for himself. The gloss more often confuses, as when it claims, at the end of Part II, that the Polar Spirit and its 'fellow-daemons' are neo-Platonic spirits—information Coleridge evidently found in Thomas Burnet in 1801 (*CN* 1,000H), since he quotes Burnet in the epigraph he later added to the poem in *Sibylline Leaves*. According to the gloss they are 'invisible inhabitants of this planet, neither departed souls nor angels' but of intermediate rank—in which case they are products of rather too learned an imagination to be in place in a popular medieval ballad. Without the gloss, they could have been accepted without difficulty as supernatural in a simpler sense. And some of the notes are not explanatory at all, but stylistic exercises in an extinct mode of English prose that Coleridge loved, like this exquisite imitation of the language of Jeremy Taylor:

> In his loneliness and fixedness he yearneth towards the journeying Moon, and the stars that still sojourn, yet still move onward; and every where the blue sky belongs to them, and is their appointed rest, and their native country and their own natural homes, which they enter unannounced, as lords that are certainly expected and yet there is a silent joy at their arrival (Part IV).

The gloss, then, is neither a parody in any specific sense, nor yet an explanation. What other function can it have? I suggest that the purpose and effect of the gloss can only be to intensify the historical, dramatic, 'as-if' element in the poem, both in the action of the poem and in its stated morality. Its effect is deliberately to enlarge doubt concerning what the Mariner says, to remind the reader that, in spite of the textual modernization of *1800*, the poem is an historical exercise which asks not to be taken literally. Coleridge, in a manner almost too ingenious, has on this occasion insisted that we should feel the gap of centuries. His first design may have been for a gloss in English as contemporary as that of the Argument of 1798, since a copy of *1800* survives containing a first draft to a gloss to Part V (ll. 345 f.):

> By the interception of his kind saint [cf. l. 286] a choir of angels

desc[ended] from Heaven, & entered into the dead bod[ies], using the bodies a[s] material Instrum[ents].[2]

In *1817*, this is jacobeanized into:

But not by the souls of the men, nor by daemons of earth or middle air, but by a blessed troop of angelic spirits, sent down by the invocation of the guardian saint.

Between the date of the pretended action (*c.* 1500), then, and the date of composition (*c.* 1800) falls, just halfway, a pretended commentary (*c.* 1650). The action, by a device scarcely to be paralleled in literature, is seen through a double historical lens. And this conclusion will prove important if it is given full weight in asking what the poem is about.

Coleridge was as suspicious as Keats of poetry that has a 'palpable design' upon us, of what he called the vice of 'metaphysical solution in poetry' (*CN* 673), or philosophy weakly dissolved in poetic language. This is the aversion that underlies his reply to Mrs Barbauld, made only a few years before his death (31 May 1830) and reported by his nephew in *Table Talk*. When Mrs Barbauld complained that the 'Mariner' was 'improbable, and had no moral', Coleridge is said to have answered 'that in my own judgement the poem had too much; and that the only, or chief fault, if I may say so, was the obtrusion of the moral sentiment so openly on the reader as a principle or cause of action in a work of such pure imagination.' Or, as Henry Nelson Coleridge reported the same exchange in an article in the *Quarterly* which appeared a week or two after the poet's death (August 1834), 'I ought not to have stopped to give reasons for things,' the poet going on to declare that there ought to have been no more explicit moral than in one of the Arabian Nights. It seems natural to suppose that this mainly refers to the conclusion of the poem, 'He prayeth best who loveth best . . .', and in the light of Coleridge's insistence it is clear that

[2] Cf. R. C. Bald, *Times Literary Supplement* (26 July 1934). The mutilated copy is in the Melbourne Public Library, and also includes an addition to the 1800 Argument, which suggests Coleridge may first have considered a longer head-summary rather than a marginal gloss.

this passage must be seen as studiously *simpliste*—not Coleridge's view, but the view of the Mariner and of the supposed author of the gloss, who chimes in obediently: 'to teach, by his own example, love and reverence to all things that God made and loveth'. To go further, the passage is not even accurate in its representation of the moral of the poem; for if the 'Mariner' had a mere Christian commonplace for its theme it would surely seem simpler and less arresting than it does. The clearest evidence is the reaction of the Wedding Guest. The Mariner's moral, 'He prayeth best who loveth best . . .', is not depressing or even discouraging, and not, in itself, out of keeping with the mood of a wedding celebration. But the Wedding Guest, on hearing it, simply cannot face the party; 'He went like one that hath been stunned,' and he wakes up next morning 'sadder and wiser'—the very fate which, in the first version of the poem, the Mariner had threatened him with:

> 'Never sadder tale was told
> To a man of woman born:
> Sadder and wiser thou wedding-guest!
> Thou'lt rise tomorrow morn.'

If the story is 'saddening', as it is, and its stated moral is not, then the moral can hardly fit the story.

There have been plenty of bids to supply a better moral than the Mariner's own. E. M. W. Tillyard, in his *Five Poems* (1948), suggested that the poem is about intellectual discovery by a 'mental voyager', that the Mariner is a kind of medievalized Coleridge or an 'enquiring spirit'; and Mr W. H. Auden, in *The Enchafèd Flood* (1950), has called the Mariner a heroic voyager 'whose dedicated career is the exploration of the hitherto unknown'. These are arresting interpretations, but they will hardly do. The Mariner's motives are never described, but it is quite clear he never wanted to get as near to the South Pole as he did, and he may not have wanted to visit the Pacific at all. He is an almost totally passive figure, as Wordsworth complained in a rather ungracious note to the second edition of *Lyrical Ballads*, and he acts only three times —in shooting the albatross, in blessing the water-snakes, and in biting his arm. And only the last of the three can be called a purposeful act—the other two actions seem as nearly purposeless as human action can be. The reader is blatantly offered no motive for his sin ('With my cross-bow I shot the albatross') and the blessing of the water-snakes is explicitly 'unaware'. The Mariner is surely no enquiring spirit: he is more like the plaything of Fate.

Another fashionable view is that the poem is about sin and redemption—and here, of course, the initial fact is much exploited: Coleridge wrote the poem 'instead' of writing 'The Wanderings of Cain'. As Cain killed Abel, according to this account, so did the Mariner kill the albatross. But this, too, is ultimately unconvincing, though the Cain analogy is mildly helpful. For the Mariner had no reason for killing the bird; Cain has a very convincing reason, though an evil one, for killing his brother. Genesis 4 tells how God respected Abel's offerings of the firstlings of the flock, but not Cain's 'fruit of the ground', and told him he must do better: 'If thou doest well, shalt thou not be accepted?' Cain's sin is explicable —it is brotherly jealousy—and he is punished by the barrenness of his land and sent forth to wander. As a sin, it bears no relation to the Mariner's, being purposeful and explicable. But Cain's punishment does. For he becomes an outlaw whom no man may kill: 'Whosoever slayeth Cain [says the Lord], vengeance shall be taken on him sevenfold. And the Lord set a mark upon Cain, lest any finding him should kill him.' In 'The Wanderings of Cain', which is composed as a melodramatic, even Gothic, imitation of biblical prose, Cain wanders hopelessly with his son in search of his own extinction, crying bitterly 'I desire to die'; 'and his countenance told in a strange and terrible language of agonies that had been, and were, and were still to continue to be.' At the end of the fragment he tells the spectre of his brother Abel, who now haunts him, that he cannot speak to God: 'I have prayed, and have not been heard' (*CPW* 288-92). This is strikingly like the fate of the Mariner: he too is condemned to live with his crime. It is punishment by life. In Part III a ghost-ship draws up to the Mariner's, and Life-in-Death gambles for the Mariner with Death itself, and wins him. The Mariner, in fact, is not to be allowed to escape his predicament. And the facts of this living predicament are then rammed home: his two hundred companions, dying of thirst on

the becalmed ocean, curse the Mariner with their eyes, and die—
and each death reminds him of the arrow he fired at the albatross.

The 'Life-in-Death' punishment of the Mariner, then, bears a
resemblance to the punishment visited by God on Cain. And those
who see the poem as essentially a Christian poem about sin and
redemption have a second trump to play: the fact that the Mariner
is saved through an act of charity, in blessing the water-snakes.
Charity is the supreme Christian virtue; and some of Coleridge's
language ('The self-same moment I could pray') does sound very
like a good deal of devotional literature: the Mariner first hardens
his heart towards God and cannot pray, like King Claudius in
*Hamlet* but, unlike Claudius, is released by an act of divine mercy
('Sure my kind saint took pity on me'). And yet it is not convincing.
The emphasis, which is no more heretical than that of many key
passages about spiritual revelation in Wordsworth's *Prelude*, is
surely too idiosyncratic, in ordinary theological terms, to be allowed.
And it is idiosyncratic in just the same way as the *Prelude*:

> To the brim
> My heart was full; I made no vows, but vows
> Were then made for me; bond unknown to me
> Was given . . . (1805 *Prelude*, iv 340-3).

The point of emphasis is not that the Mariner sins and repents—
though this, of course, is not false—but that both sin and repentance
are visited upon him. The Mariner is simply not felt to be morally
responsible, as he would be in any ordinary Christian parable.
Indeed his passivity is insisted upon. If this is a Christian parable,
then it is an oddly quietistic form of Christianity.

This is not a matter of biographical inference. Coleridge's
religious views are well enough known: how he passed from
Anglicanism to Unitarianism at Cambridge in the early 1790's and
back again before his return to England in 1806. The Gutch notebook of 1795-7, written at the beginning of his great burst of poetic
energy, suggests that his interest in prayer was an active one, and
that it bears a relationship to the Mariner's own experience (*CN*
257), for Coleridge there distinguishes five stages of prayer, from
'the pressure of immediate calamities' to 'horrible solitude', 'repent-

ance and regret', 'celestial delectation', and finally 'self-annihilation'. A note scribbed in a copy of Kant confirms a natural suspicion that, at this point of the poem at least, an issue of deep personal conviction is at stake: 'Who ever prayed that has not an hundred times felt that scarce an act of life was so difficult as to determine to pray?' De Quincey confirmed the point shortly after Coleridge's death: 'He told me as his own particular opinion that the act of praying was the very highest energy of which the human heart was capable; praying, that is, with the total concentration of the faculties.'[3]

But to concede that the 'Mariner' has a Christian dimension still allows for the view that the sin-redemption theory, while superficially attractive, leaves too much evidence out. Indeed its superficial aptness is the worst thing about it. A moment ago I spoke of 'Coleridge's language' reminding us of devotional literature. But of course, in a significant sense, this is not Coleridge's language at all: it is the Ancient Mariner's. Coleridge made two attempts to impress upon the reader the fact that it is not his own. First, he cast the whole poem into medieval language, spelling and metre; and secondly when, after complaints about obscurity, he had modernized the spelling and some of the language too, he added a gloss which just as obviously is not 'Coleridge's language' either, but the language of some remote antiquary. And finally, thirty years later, he regretted in conversation 'the obtrusion of the moral sentiment'. The evidence is not quite conclusive, but it is very strong: Coleridge is eager to make clear that the poem is not *in propria persona*, that the moral commentary he has put into the mouth of the Mariner is not, for him, the point of the poem. This too is an aspect of his 1797 pact with Wordsworth: Coleridge's 'incidents and agents were to be, in part at least, supernatural; and the excellence aimed at was to consist in the interesting of the affections by the dramatic truth of such emotions as would naturally accompany such situations, supposing them real' (*BL* xiv). The very fault of 'predilection for the dramatic form' of which Coleridge later accused Wordsworth (*BL* xxii), is fully characteristic of his own contribution

[3] *Tait's Magazine* (Sept. 1834); *Collected Writings*, ed. David Masson, Edinburgh (1889-90), vol. ii, p. 157.

to the *Lyrical Ballads*, and the dramatic force of the poem is a thing to be neglected only at peril. The Mariner's moral is a centrally Christian one: 'He prayeth best who loveth best.' But there is no certainty or even probability that it is Coleridge's. And if this is not the point of the poem, the reader may be encouraged to re-interpret the Mariner's commentary throughout: he is no more required to believe the Mariner's moral asides to be Coleridge's than to accept phrases like 'To Mary Queen the praise be given' as evidence of the poet's mariolatry during his unitarian years. The truth of the poem, like that of most of the *Lyrical Ballads*, is a dramatic truth, and the Mariner may well be wrong, with Coleridge's relation to him as remote as Wordsworth's to the 'simple child' who knows nothing of death in 'We are Seven', or to the naïvely courageous leech-gatherer in 'Resolution and Independence'. Reading the poem cultivates an awareness which Coleridge has himself tried to enforce, by the double device of ballad and gloss, of the vast historical gap between the modern English poet and Catholic Europe, and of Coleridge's own remoteness from the Mariner's inspired simplicity; and the Mariner may be no more capable of explaining what he knows than are Wordsworth's shepherds or children. His very narrative technique is probably meant to be medieval. The 'ballad romance', as Peacock observed in 1818 (though he oddly misapplied the term to 'Christabel') is 'a tale of wonder and mystery told with the simplicity of our elder minstrels, who depict every scene as it were passing under their eyes, and narrate their most marvellous legends with an unaffected *bonne foi* that shews a mind fully impressed with the truth of its own tale . . . Their language is always that of circumstantial evidence, never of complete and positive testimony.'[4] It is, in fact, an assumption of the *naïf*.

What is the 'Ancient Mariner' about? The Wordsworthian parallels I have just quoted, and indeed the place of the poem as first among the *Lyrical Ballads* and a direct product of the pact of

---

[4] 'An Essay on Fashionable Literature', a fragment first published complete, from a manuscript in the British Museum, in the Halliford edition of the *Works of Thomas Love Peacock*, edited by H. F. B. Brett-Smith and C. E. Jones, vol. viii, London (1934), p. 281.

1797, should give the clue. It is in its objectives very much a 'lyrical ballad' and a product of collaboration, however Coleridgean in the intense and elaborate erudition of its form and style. The Wordsworthian ballads of *1798* are studies in a lost simplicity, a simplicity which the poor, the insane, and the very young possess, but which the educated man and the poet have been unable since childhood to enjoy; and the last of them, the 'Lines Composed a Few Miles above Tintern Abbey', which Wordsworth wrote as late as June 1798, a few weeks before the collection appeared, concludes the book with an unexpected and even incongruous explicitness. It is in blank verse, it is manifestly no sort of ballad, lyrical or other, it eschews the dramatic and openly tells us what to think. Any doubts concerning the unifying principle of *1798* are dispelled here, in this passionate coda proclaiming the principle of human growth, of the passage from innocence into experience (as Blake had recently put it), from the unthinking, animal felicity of youth to the intellecualism and limited sensitivity of the grown man. Lamb, who may have been the most perceptive reader Coleridge ever had, as he was certainly the best informed concerning the private elements involved in his poetry, saw at once that the chief realities of the poem were psychological. 'The Ancient Mariner', he wrote to Wordsworth in January 1801, 'undergoes such trials as overwhelm and bury all individuality: . . . all consciousness of personality is gone.' The re-making of the human personality under the flux of time is the great matter of *Lyrical Ballads*. And it is surely a matter of real, if mysterious, significance that when Coleridge, in the last year of his life, came to write an epitaph, he inverted the phrase 'Life-in-Death' to apply to his own case:

> That he who many year with toil of breath
> Found death in life, may here find life in death! (*CPW* 492);

and in 'Constancy to an Ideal Object' he was to compare his loveless plight with one in a 'becalmed bark'

> Whose Helmsman on an ocean waste and wide
> Sits mute and pale his mouldering helm beside (*CPW* 456).

In a note written in his middle years, too, he varies the same favourite analogy. 'I would compare the human soul to a ship's crew cast on an unknown island' (*CN* 3,484).

And yet the 'Mariner', like the Dejection Ode of 1802, remains a whole world away from 'Tintern Abbey'. The difference lies in the simple fact that Coleridge knows what it is to lose, and he knows that no imaginable recompense will do: no recompense, certainly, for the sensitivity of response that could 'feel' as well as 'see', that had lived in the body like Wordsworth's appetite of youth:

> a feeling and a love
> That had no need of a remoter charm,
> By thought supplied, nor any interest
> Unborrowed from the eye (ll. 80-3).

Read the 'Mariner' in the light of a truth which the two poets shared and reflected upon at the moment when, in their mid-twenties, they may themselves have lived through the loss of such virtue, and one perceives a new coherence in the collection which together they planned and executed. It is also to find a key that opens doors, that justifies the principal details of the 'Mariner' itself. For the Mariner, like the Wordsworth of 'Tintern Abbey' and of the *Prelude*, has lived through a spiritual revolution, and one which visited itself upon him through no will of his. Part I of the poem, in the merry departure from port, the fast driving of the ship before the storm-blast, and the good luck brought by the Albatross, tells of a world like Wordsworth's youthful felicity, and its loss is as unaccountable as his:

> With my cross-bow
> I shot the Albatross.

Innocence is lost as effortlessly and irresistibly as Natural Man loses it in the act of growing up. Public opinion, education, indeed all human environment, prove impotent at the tragic moment when innocence dies, as they do for the Wordsworthian recluse—hence the contemptible behaviour of the Mariner's companions in Part II, who vacillate disgracefully over the shooting of the bird:

H

> And I had done a hellish thing,
> And it would work 'em woe:
> For all averred, I had killed the bird
> That made the breeze to blow.
> Ah wretch! said they, the bird to slay
> That made the breeze to blow!
>
> Nor dim nor red, like God's own head
> The glorious Sun uprist:
> Then all averred, I had killed the bird
> That brought the fog and mist.
> 'Twas right, said they, such birds to slay
> That bring the fog and mist.

Others are useless, and salvation can only be found alone. The Mariner is alone by Part IV, after his two hundred shipmates have dropped down dead, 'on a wide wide sea'; and here, in the darkly magnificent and purgatorial phase of the poem, the punishment of Life-in-Death is luridly played out, packed with nightmarish effects utterly unWordsworthian—'This body dropped not down'— and a large return for the contract by which Wordsworth had ceded to his friend the realm of the supernatural. The Mariner's punishment is perhaps the finest dramatic portrait of self-disgust in English since *Hamlet*; but whereas Hamlet mourns his incapacity to love the world as it deserves to be loved ('Man delights not me'), the Mariner, like a medieval penitent, is consumed by a sense of his own unworthiness before the reproach of a world of beauty he is morally unfit to inhabit:

> The many men, so beautiful!
> And they all dead did lie:
> And a thousand thousand slimy things
> Lived on; and so did I.

This intensely dramatized hysteria of horror, where the poem comes so near to screaming-point, is the climax of Coleridge's achievement during the vital year of 1797-8, and stands in utter opposition to the careful analytical tone of much of the conversation poems that he composed before, during and after. It is also true that nightmare, simply because it is so heavily dramatized, is easier to bear than the 'thought without a pang, void, dark, and drear' of the Dejection Ode. Dramatization can be anaesthetic. When, as befits a poem composed in the full flush of intimacy with Wordsworthian optimism, the nightmare ends and the spirit is re-animated, Coleridge's very language at the moment when the Mariner watches the water-snakes echoes a Wordsworthian commonplace:

> A spring of love gushed from my heart,
> And I blessed them unaware,

The first line of the *Prelude* runs: 'Oh there is blessing in this gentle breeze.' Nature heals the man who makes no effort but simply opens himself, 'unaware', to its influence. Now the world returns, but in ghostly fashion, in the spiritual convalescence of Part V, and the Mariner's shipmates are brought back to a kind of life:

> They groaned, they stirred, they all uprose,
> Nor spake, nor moved their eyes,

since, in the new existence, experience is no longer 'animal', as in youth, but spiritual or angelic:

> Each corse lay flat, lifeless and flat,
> And, by the holy rood!
> A man all light, a seraph-man,
> On every corse there stood,

and the Mariner, in the 'return' of the poem, sails into harbour to review the home port described in Part I, in a pattern that reflects the movement of the conversation poems; and sees it now no longer steeped in sunshine and holiday mood, but of a silent, ghostly beauty lost to all that is human and sensual, eerily bright and inviting only dispassionate praise:

> The harbour-bay was clear as glass,
> So smoothly it was strewn!

> And on the bay the moonlight lay,
> And the shadow of the Moon.
>
> The rock shone bright, the kirk no less,
> That stands above the rock:
> The moonlight steeped in silentness
> The steady weathercock.
>
> And the bay was white with silent light,
> Till rising from the same,
> Full many shapes, that shadows were,
> In crimson colours came.

The ghostly return of the shipmates to another life as a seraph-band echoes Coleridge's fascination with memory and the tricks it plays to reveal change in oneself. This is how he described his return to Cambridge in a note of October 1806, looking on a city he had not seen since he had left it as a student twelve years before: 'Every thing the same—thereby distinguished in its effect on the feelings from the scenes of childhood visited in manhood, which all seem ludicrously small. The young men seemed the very same young men I had left . . . The only alteration in myself' (*CN* 2,894). Shortly after, he tried to explain how it was:

> Memory, a wan misery-eyed female, . . . fed on bitter fruits from the Tree of Life—and often she attempted to tear off from her forehead a seal which eternity had placed there; and instantly she found in her hand a hideous phantom of her own visage, with that seal on its forehead; and as she stood horror-struck, beholding the phantom-head so wan and supernatural, which she seemed to hold before her eyes, with right hand too numb or feel or be felt . . . the vision enriched by subconsciousness of palpability, by influent recollections of touch (*CN* 2,915).

Like the 'Ancient Mariner' itself, this is a spectre-vision of an encounter across a waste of time, and of that infinite loss mourned or celebrated by other Lyrical Ballads: the loss of appetite and youth.

# CHAPTER SEVEN

# Christabel

Coleridge's omission to finish 'Christabel', which survives as a bulky torso of 677 lines, has often been held to mark his ultimate failure as a poet. And there can be no doubt that the failure was humiliating to the poet himself. If only for his own peace of mind, an author cannot allow himself to be defeated in this way, and Coleridge's repeated attempts to finish the poem, the accounts of its conclusion that he made to members of his circle, and the defiant claims he made at the end of his life that 'I have, as I always had, the whole plan entire from beginning to end in my mind',[1] all suggests something alarmingly like a loss of nerve. Still, it hardly follows that the undertaking was ill judged or that the difficulties of completing it were weighty. In the delicate profession of poetry a loss of nerve can arise from no reason at all. From no poetic reason, that is—Coleridge's increasing self-abasement after the turn of the century before Wordsworth's more fertile genius, and his awareness as their friendship waned that 'Christabel', like 'The Ancient Mariner', had owed everything to their collaboration in *Lyrical Ballads* during the years 1797-8, may have created a sense of anxiety too deep and too obscure ever to be stilled.

The known facts of the composition of 'Christabel', which are more speculative than certain, suggest how deeply collaborative an enterprise the poem was. When Coleridge first came to publish it years later in 1816, in a pamphlet which included 'Kubla Khan' and 'The Pains of Sleep', he added a preface claiming that 'the first part of the following poem was written in the year 1797, at Stowey, in the county of Somerset. The second part, after my return from Germany, in the year 1800, at Keswick, Cumberland'

[1] *Table Talk* (6 July 1833), a year before his death.

(*CPW* 213). Wordsworth, who is an earlier witness, writes in the *Prelude* of 1805 as if 'Christabel' and the 'Mariner' were broadly simultaneous compositions of 1798:

> That summer when on Quantock's grassy hills
> Far ranging, and among the sylvan coombs,
> Thou in delicious words, with happy heart,
> Didst speak the Vision of that Ancient Man,
> The bright-eyed Mariner, and rueful woes
> Didst utter of the Lady Christabel . . . (xiii 393-8).

Dorothy Wordsworth's journal, which early in 1798 includes phrases evidently borrowed by Coleridge for the poem, offers solider evidence for supposing that Part I of 'Christabel' was written in 1798: while Part II of the poem—and perhaps the brief conclusion to the first part as well—were clearly written after the return from Germany at Keswick, in the autumn of 1800 and after, in a vain attempt to complete the poem for the second edition of *Lyrical Ballads* in the same year. Such a disturbed history might be expected to do violence to the unity of the poem, and so it does. The conclusion to Part II, where the poem finally breaks off ('A little child, a limber elf . . .'), sent in a letter to Southey on 6 May 1801 (*CL* ii 728), is an affectionate tribute to the three-year old infant Hartley which has little demonstrable connection with the rest of the poem, though the 'sweet recoil of love and pity' (l. 672) might refer to Sir Leoline's rejection of his daughter Christabel when she begs him to send Geraldine away. But even the relation between the two major parts, divided as they were by the year in Germany (1798-9), is not as close as it needs to be. The first part excels in effects of the vividly present ("'Tis the middle of night by the castle clock . . .'), the reader being cast in the role of the mystified spectator; the second is more conventionally narrative. It seems likely that Coleridge not only changed his mind in later years about how to finish the poem, but that even the fragment that survives is not altogether of a piece.

Such reflections should give pause to speculation, and hesitation might well be advised in any case. To enquire for long about how Coleridge would have finished his poem is hardly a reasonable exercise. Criticism is about what is, not about what might have been. Dr Gillman's circumstantial account, in his *Life of Coleridge* (1838), of how the mysterious Geraldine, having turned herself into Christabel's lover, was to be unmasked at the wedding by the return of the lover himself, is not incompatible with the poem that we have; and Nethercot's hypothesis in *The Road to Tryermaine* (1939) that Geraldine is a serpent-spirit or lamia who, vampire-like, sucks the blood of her victims is altogether plausible too, in view of her 'serpent's eye' (l. 585). My concern, however, is with the poem that exists. My task here is the unfulfilled double task that Coleridge set himself in a letter to Poole in March 1801, when he proposed to publish the poem 'with two essays annexed to it, on the Praeternatural and on Metre' (*CL* ii 707). It is not really the plot that holds attention in 'Christabel'. The metre of the poem, and the function of the supernatural within it, are the prime aspects of its compelling power.

Coleridge's intense fascination with the metres of classical and modern poetry was continuous from his earliest experiments as a poet, and 'Christabel' represents the most daring experiment of all. Wordsworth reported that Coleridge bestowed inconceivable labour when he was 'intent on a new experiment in metre', and that he was 'quite an epicure in sound'; and his daughter Sara once wrote to a friend that, in his later days, Coleridge 'was fond of talking about anapaests and iambuses; and if people admired "Christabel", as it were, by nature, he was never easy till he had put them in the way of admiring it more scientifically'.[2] At the age of twenty-four he was already turning from classical imitation to modern, and employed his knowledge of the classical languages, which was excellent if indifferent to detail, by anonymously reviewing Samuel Horsley's pamphlet *On the Prosodies of the Greek and Latin Languages* (1796) in the *Critical Review* (February 1797). He remarked there, following Bishop Horsley, that English 'differs in

[2] Mr Justice Coleridge, in Christopher Wordsworth, *Memoirs of Wordsworth*, London (1851), vol. ii, p. 306; Sara Coleridge, *Memoir and Letters*, ed. Edith Coleridge, London (1873), vol. i, pp. 307-8; and for some of Coleridge's metrical examples *CPW* 1,014-20 (with notes by George Saintsbury), though few or none of these poems, as is now known, are in fact by Coleridge.

the powers of the vowels from every other language upon earth'—a
dubious statement if it means that English differs radically from
other Germanic languages in its metrical properties, but more
probably intended as a sensible reminder that English accent is
not Latin quantity. By the late 1790's Coleridge's interest in metre
had grown into a passion to extend the range of English by liberat-
ing it from the classical heritage and encouraging it to borrow
from German and Italian sources. German, being a compound-
forming language, he thought to possess a certain advantage over
English 'in the imitation of the ancient metres' (*CN* 3,474). Given
the nature of the English language, the classics are largely a dead
end. But to reject the classics is not to reject all deliberation on the
subject. The daring metrical ingenuities of the great poems of
1797-8 show how little, even at the height of his intimacy with
Wordsworth, Coleridge accepted the notion of Wordsworth's 1800
preface that metre was a mere additional charm, 'superadded' and
'adventitious'. In 'The Ancient Mariner' ballad-metre had been
an indispensable aspect of historical remoteness, and the poem is
unimaginable in any other form. In 'Christabel' the metre is not
nostalgic, but rather novel and experimental, and forces itself for
just this reason upon the fascinated attention of the reader. No
greater contrast with the conversation poems is conceivable. It is as
if Coleridge recognized within two or three years of 'The Eolian
Harp' that the quiet, blank-verse meditative tradition of Cowper
and Lamb was a programme for adequacy but not for excellence.
'An affectation of plainness and simplicity,' as he copied from an
anonymous review in January 1804, 'is the flimsiest covering for
incapacity that was ever assumed' (*CN* 1848), and a dozen years
later he expounded a formal theory of metre as a 'salutary antagon-
ism' between discipline and passion (*BL* xviii). But, like much of
his criticism, all this is a slow and painful exploration of something
he had already triumphantly done.

The 1816 preface to 'Christabel' offers a summary account and
justification of the metre of the poem:

> the metre of 'Christabel' is not, properly speaking, irregular, though
> it may seem so from its being founded on a new principle: namely,

that of counting in each line the accents, not the syllables. Though the latter may vary from seven to twelve, yet in each line the accent will be found to be only four (*CPW* 215),

and Coleridge adds that the variations are not 'wanton', but rather 'in correspondence with some transition in the nature of the imagery or passion'. This account is accurate in a high degree. In a fragment of well over 600 lines, only sixteen violate the principle of four accents distributed among seven to twelve syllables. Coleridge has been thought to have a little exaggerated the originality of his metre: in fact about four-fifths of the lines are conventional iambic four-footers, usually in rhyming couplets, and it might be argued that the variations in the remaining fifth are already familiar in English verse, being no more than a matter of extra unaccented syllables. But Coleridge's large claim is justified by the total effect of the poem. If other English poems in rhyming four-footers are put beside it, such as Crashaw's 'St Theresa' (1646), which Coleridge later claimed had been 'ever present to my mind whilst writing the second part of Christabel' and which had perhaps suggested the whole poem,[3] or Marvell's 'Coy Mistress' (1681), or Burns's *Tam O'Shanter* (1795), the difference between an occasional licence and a mannerism deliberately exploited is clear at once. There had been nothing before in English poetry like

> There is not wind enough to twirl
> The one red leaf, the last of its clan,
> That dances as often as dance it can,
> Hanging so light, and hanging so high,
> On the topmost twig that looks up at the sky (ll. 48-52),

a passage to justify Coleridge's claim that the metre of this poem can stir into novelty 'in correspondence with some transition' in the movement of the poem itself. Such delicate impressionism of rhythm was hard to learn, and English poets did not learn it for half a century or more. Scott and Byron knew the poem in manuscript years before it was published, or had heard it recited; but their attempts to imitate its metre only show how much was still left to

[3] Allsop, *Letters, Conversations and Recollections of Coleridge*, London (1836), I. 194-6.

achieve. Scott's *Lay of the Last Minstrel* (1805) catches some of the excitement of an incantation, but in his hands the metre turns into a rattle that is too even and repetitious ever to achieve subtlety:

> The feast was over in Branksome tower,
> And the Ladye had gone to her secret bower;
> Her bower that was guarded by word and by spell,
> Deadly to hear, and deadly to tell—
> Jesu Maria, shield us well! (I. 1-5).

Byron in the *Siege of Corinth* (1816), a poem published early in the same year as 'Christabel', acknowledged an unintentional debt to Coleridge in a note to the following passage; but he achieved only a hint of Coleridgean subtlety, with little of its aptness:

> Was it the wind through some hollow stone
> Sent that soft and tender moan?
> He lifted his head, and he look'd on the sea,
> But it was unrippled as glass may be;
> He look'd on the long grass—it waved not a blade . . .
>
> (ll. 521-5).

The real successors to 'Christabel' are not direct metrical successors like the poems of Scott or of Byron, but rather Keats's 'Eve of St Agnes' (1820), which is in Spenserian stanzas, and certain mid-Victorian peoms that, like Keats's, owe to it more remotely and obliquely—poems that have nothing to do with the rhyming four-footer. Some of the subtlest of Tennyson's metrical effects, or Swinburne's, where the tyranny of the two-syllable foot is altogether abandoned, may be part of the true legacy:

> My dust would hear her and beat
> Had I lain for a century dead;
> Would start and tremble under her feet,
> And blossom in purple and red.

The 'praeternatural', or supernatural aspects of 'Christabel' are, in its unfinished state, more difficult to determine. The resemblance of the poem to a Gothic romance was noticed as soon as the poem appeared, and even before: an anonymous parody entitled 'Christoball: a Gothic Tale', appeared in the *European Magazine* in April 1815; and H. N. Coleridge, in his article in the *Quarterly* of 1834, memorably defined the peculiar quality of the poem in a phrase that seems to take its kinship with the Gothic for granted: 'the thing attempted in "Christabel" is the most difficult of execution in the whole field of romance—witchery by daylight'. He seems to have supposed that Coleridge's achievement was to bring the Gothic tale out of the vault, the charnel-house, the cavern and candle-lit castle into the light of the sun. This is indeed just what is happening in 'Christabel'; and it is fitting that Coleridge, who may have begun reviewing Gothic novels in the *Critical Review* at the age of twenty-one with a welcoming notice of Mrs Radcliffe's *Udolpho* (1794), should have turned to the form for a poetic exercise that might fulfil his share of *Lyrical Ballads*. The Gothic novel, by the 1790's, was something much more than a dominant form for the supernatural —it had come near, in the first years of the Regency, to ranking as the form dominant in all popular literature. When Coleridge was a boy it was already offering the English common reader an imaginative relationship with the European past more complicated and diverse than its progenitor, Horace Walpole, can ever have dreamed of. In the 1760's, it is true, the Middle Ages had been rapidly annexed to the English literary imagination with Ossian (1760-3), Hurd's *Letters on Chivalry and Romance* (1762), Percy's *Reliques* (1765) and Walpole's *The Castle of Otranto* (1765). But the remote past had been offered then as a point of rest rather than of departure. The Middle Ages, at this first stage of the Gothic revival, were for day-dreams and wish-fulfilments. 'Old castles, old pictures, old histories, and the babble of old people make one live back into centuries that cannot disappoint one', Walpole wrote to a friend about a year after his novel appeared. 'One holds fast and surely what is past. The dead have exhausted their power of deceiving . . .'[4] They have certainly regained that power by the end of the century. Walpole's attempt to reconcile gentility with horror, 'to blend the two kinds of romance, the ancient and the modern', as he put it in

---

[4] Letter to George Montagu (5 Jan. 1766); *Horace Walpole's Correspondence with George Montagu*, ed. W. S. Lewis and R. S. Brown, New Haven (1941), vol. ii, p. 192.

his preface to the second edition of *Otranto*, had by the 1790's tended to diverge, though never widely, into two streams: the genteel novels of Coleridge's favourite of the Gothic school, Mrs Radcliffe, which stand in the ancestral line of the late Victorian and twentieth-century detective story, where the horrors only seem supernatural and are rapidly shown to have natural causes; and the novel of sheer terror, uninhibitedly supernatural and often with German sources, like M. G. Lewis's *Monk* (1796). Coleridge recognized this distinction in his early reviews. Mrs Radcliffe's art, which he admired, lay in 'concealing her plan with the most artificial contrivance,' so that the authoress 'seems to amuse herself with saying, at every turn and doubling of the story, "Now you think you have me, but I shall take care to disappoint you".' The gratuitous horror of *The Monk*, on the other hand, and especially its abundant prurience, shocked him to the core: 'Situations of torment, and images of naked horror, are easily conceived; and a writer in whose works they abound deserves our gratitude almost equally with him who should drag us by way of sport through a military hospital, or force us to sit at the dissecting-table . . .'[5] The Gothic in fiction was to begin its decline in the first decade of the nineteenth century, and was largely defeated by the historical reality of the Waverley novels after 1814; but it was near the very climax of its vogue in the late 1790's, when it was the subject of two great pastiches, each more memorable by far than the works it imitates. The one is 'Christabel' itself, the other Jane Austen's *Northanger Abbey* (1818), which was exactly contemporaneous with Coleridge's poem, being largely written in 1797-8 and completed by 1803, though (like the poem) it did not appear until after Waterloo. The parallel is even closer. *Northanger Abbey*, whatever its later reputation, is hardly a satire upon the Gothic. It is rather, at the worst, an indulgently ironic glance at the state of fiction at the time of composition. It includes, at the end of the fifth chapter, a passionate attack upon the detraction of current fiction, upon the 'common

---

[5] From the reviews of *Udolpho* and *The Monk* in the *Critical Review* (August 1794 and February 1797); *Coleridge's Miscellaneous Criticism*, ed. T. M. Raysor, Cambridge, Mass. (1936), pp. 356, 372. Cf. his remark in a later note on 'the vicious taste of our modern Radcliffe, Monk Lewis' (*CN* 3,473).

cant' of condescending remarks such as 'It is only a novel'. The heroine's anti-climactic discovery, at the beginning of a later chapter, that the papers she had been forced in terror to leave un-read on her bedroom floor on the previous night were nothing but washing-bills, can hardly represent a satirical view of Mrs Radcliffe, who knowingly employs the same device of self-deflation over and over again; though it is true that in Jane Austen the situation is played more openly for comic effect. It seems altogether likely that Coleridge and Jane Austen both genuinely admired the Gothic romance while deploring its excesses; and 'Christabel', a story of sexual molestation and terrorism practised upon a virgin by a super-natural power, seems to accept without irony the serious task of chilling the reader's spine. In some major respects, indeed, 'Christa-bel' is more like the condemned *Monk* than the admired *Udolpho*. As in Lewis's novel, the supernatural in 'Christabel' is genuinely there—it is surely not a mere illusion to be exposed at the end, as in a Radcliffe novel. And no explanation can deprive the reader of his fear before the nameless sexuality of the mysterious Geraldine, who with bared bosom and a side that is 'a sight to dream of, not to tell', lays herself beside the innocent Christabel with these words:

> 'In the touch of this bosom there worketh a spell,
> Which is lord of thy utterance, Christabel!
> Thou knowest to-night, and wilt know to-morrow,
> This mark of my shame, this seal of my sorrow . . .' (ll. 267-70)

All this seems a long way outside the genteel range of Mrs Radcliffe.

One trick of Gothic language Coleridge and Jane Austen both accepted: the trick of using a series of unanswered and, for the time being, unanswerable questions, massed together in nervous repetition to heighten suspense. The trick is so natural to any literary form that depends for its chief effect upon building a sense of fore-boding that it is unexpected to find how little Mrs Radcliffe and Lewis employ it in narrative, though they often exploit it in dialogue. ' "You here, Matilda!" ' cries Lewis's monk to his accomplice in the last chapter of the novel, after he has raped and murdered the beautiful Antonia. ' "How have you gained entrance? Where are your chains? What means this magnificence, and the joy which sparkles in your eyes? Have our judges relented? Is there a chance of my escaping?"' Schedoni, the evil priest in Mrs Radcliffe's *The Italian* (1797), talks the same language when he is on the point of stabbing the sleeping Ellena: '"Do I not feel the necessity of this act! Does not what is dearer to me than existence—does not my consequence depend on the execution of it? Is she not also beloved by the young Vivaldi?—have I already forgotten the church of the Spirito Santo?"' This passage, which is quoted by Coleridge in his review of *The Italian* in the *Critical Review* (June 1798), is representative of the naggingly nervous style of Regency tales of terror which Jane Austen echoes in *Northanger Abbey* at the moment when her heroine finds the mysterious paper:

> . . . how was it to be accounted for?—What could it contain?— to whom could it relate?—by what means could it have been so long concealed?—and how singularly strange that it should fall to her lot to discover it! (ch. xxi)

At the beginning of 'Christabel', the same device is employed to identify the literary kind; and no contemporary reader need have had much difficulty, with the addition of so much medieval detail, in recognizing the poem as a Gothic tale in verse:

> Is the night chilly and dark?
> The night is chilly, but not dark . . .

> What makes her in the wood so late,
> A furlong from the castle gate? . . .

> For what can ail the mastiff bitch?

The essential purpose of 'Christabel', then, does not seem mysterious at all: it is a poem of Gothic terror. If it is not the first in English, it is certainly the first in which the critical and metrical sense was lively and original enough to offer a hope of success. The Gothic poem as such can hardly have seemed an oddity by the 1790's; as early as the 1770's the young William Blake had written 'Fair Elenor', a blank-verse narrative Coleridge was unlikely to have known, where a wife hears the name of her husband's murderer from the lips of his severed head. When it is considered how many remote literary forms Coleridge had already employed by 1798, the choice of the rising vogue of the Gothic romance seems a heavily obvious one. The familiarity of the enterprise, indeed, is perhaps what killed it. Anyone, and especially Coleridge, could think of a hundred ways of ending such a story, each one more horrific than the last; and if, in some moods, he thought it easy to do, he may also have thought it too easy to be worth doing. 'If I should finish "Christabel",' he is reported to have said in about 1820, 'I shall certainly extend it and give new characters, and a greater number of incidents. This the reading public require, and this is the reason that Sir Walter Scott's poems, though so loosely written, are pleasing, and interest us by their picturesqueness.'[6] The allusion to Scott shows how modest, at some moments, the project was: it was playing for no stakes at all. At other times he spoke as if 'the execution of the idea' were the great problem, 'an extremely subtle and difficult one.'[7] Odd as it may seem, there is perhaps no incompatibility here. A poet of genius working in an over-familiar form suffers from opposite temptations: either to behave in a familiar way, which hardly seems interesting enough to hold his attention; or to subtilize the whole undertaking ambitiously, in which case he may feel uncertain of his ability to carry it through. Coleridge's refusal to go on with 'Christabel' may have been like this. The interests offered by a new metre and a Gothic language were not slight; but after six hundred lines and more he had exhausted them both.

[6] Allsop, *Letters, Conversations and Recollections of Coleridge*, London (1836), I. 94.
[7] *Table Talk* (6 July 1833).

CHAPTER EIGHT

# Kubla Khan

Before he was twenty-six years old, and before the first edition of
*Lyrical Ballads* appeared, Coleridge had made himself a poet of
many languages: an apprentice in many styles, and already a master
of some, as 'The Ancient Mariner', 'Christabel', and 'Frost at Midnight' all variously show. He was perhaps the first European poet
to set himself the task of achieving a wide diversity of styles based
upon models other than classical ones; the undertaking, after all,
would have seemed barbarous nonsense to an Augustan, and un-
thinkable to a Renaissance poet. 'Kubla Khan' is a more difficult
case to interpret than the preceding poems, so that this chapter is
bound to be speculative; but then by the late 1790's Coleridge might
be said to have earned some right to be difficult. He was ready for
ingenious solutions. Perhaps ingenuity is too pale a word to describe
his poetic strength at this moment, at the height of his talent; but
some of his solutions, like that in the 'Mariner' of giving a medieval
dress to the most modern of themes, impress above all by their
calculation and their temerity.

All this prepares for the confession that some aspects of 'Kubla
Khan' remain inexplicable. The metre, for a start, is like nothing
at all. The matter of dating might have proved crucial here, but
unfortunately it remains inconclusive, and the traditional com-
position-date of May 1798 (*CPW* 295), which would leave the poem
just later than the 'Mariner' and probably later than the beginning
of 'Christabel', has been challenged in favour of Coleridge's own
date of 1797 and, less plausibly, in favour of 1799-1800. If the poem
is later than any part of 'Christabel', then its rhythm would represent a marked reaction back towards the heavy iambic beat of
traditional English verse:

I                                                                   117

> In Xanadu did Kubla Khan
> A stately pleasure-dome decree:
> Where Alph, the sacred river, ran
> Through caverns measureless to man
> Down to a sunless sea . . . (*CPW* 297).

The comparison with 'Christabel' is the more tempting since both poems are largely composed in four-footers; but it is impossible to explain, though easy to applaud, the strange compromise whereby 'Kubla Khan' moves in the most traditional of iambics from paragraph to paragraph in a rhyme-scheme that is always present, and yet neither stanzaic nor yet like an ode. The language of the poem is problematical too, given the bare facts that it is by Coleridge and of the 1790's. Unlike the 'Mariner' and 'Christabel', it is in contemporary English, a fact which would pose no sort of puzzle for most poems in most ages, but which is very like a suspicious circumstance here. As a matter of fact, the suspicion is justified. Coleridge's source, to which he drew attention in the preface of 1816, on first publishing the poem side by side with 'Christabel', is a source in Jacobean prose: not the richly convoluted Jacobean of Jeremy Taylor which he was to imitate in the prose gloss to the 'Mariner', but the homespun Jacobean of Hakluyt's assistant Samuel Purchas. Coleridge obligingly quotes, or rather misquotes, the passage from Purchas's *Pilgrimage* (1613) in his preface to the poem. It actually reads:

> In Xaindu did Cublai Can build a stately pallace, encompassing sixteene miles of plaine ground with a wall, wherein are fertile meddowes, pleasant springs, delightfull streames, and all sorts of beasts of chase and game, and in the middest thereof a sumptuous house of pleasure . . . (IV.xi).

It is easy to imagine what Coleridge in another mood might have made of that. In fact he rejects from it everything that is beguilingly of its period—'encompassing', 'beasts of chase and game', 'in the middest thereof'. The poem is arrantly modern. Much of it offers a kind of dynamic precision of language which is quite unlike the English of any age previous to Coleridge's:

. . . A mighty fountain momently was forced:
Amid whose swift half-intermitted burst
Huge fragments vaulted like rebounding hail,
Or chaffy grain beneath the thresher's flail.

If 'Kubla Khan' is a poem of the *annus mirabilis* of 1797-8, as still seems likely, and late rather than early in that year, then it is a striking inversion of Coleridgean formula. Instead of putting on the language of another, Coleridge has in this instance stripped it off. This is not to say that the language of the poem, or even of the first paragraph, is merely residual. It has too much life of its own for that. But its modernity is itself a device.

Such ingenuities ought to underline our uncertainty concerning the poet's purpose in 'Kubla Khan'. The fact is that almost everything is known about the poem except what it is about. Scholarship has been lavished upon the problem of dating. The very farmhouse in Culbone, a tiny village on the Somerset coast where the poet may have been interrupted in his composition, as he tells us in the 1816 preface, by 'a person on business from Porlock', has been plausibly identified. The allegedly creative effects of opium-taking have been experimentally investigated and on the whole discredited. But an interpretation of the poem that is generally acceptable is no nearer than ever. Even Humphry House in his Clark Lectures, though he called it 'a triumphant positive statement of the potentialities of poetry',[1] fumbled in his conclusion, narrowly missed the point of the poem, and failed to show how its logic works.

Taking heart from the medical evidence, which discounts the notion that opium produces either dreams in sleep or waking hallucinations, I shall dismiss one troublesome possibility at once. The Crewe manuscript of 1810, now in the British Museum, announces in Coleridge's own hand that the poem was 'composed in a sort of reverie'. By 1816, in the subtitle to the first printed version, the poem is rather bafflingly described as 'A Vision in an Dream', and the preface claims it was composed in 'a profound sleep' of about three hours. Coleridge's own accounts, then, are something less than self-consistent; but even if they had been so, it would

[1] House, *Coleridge*, London (1953), p. 116.

still be clear that 'Kubla Khan' is not in any formal sense a dream-poem, however it may have been composed. This is not to say that Coleridge's own accounts of how it came to be written are either mendacious or mistaken, though (after a lapse of a dozen years and more) it would not be surprising or disgraceful if they proved unreliable. It is simply that the poem is not a dream-poem in the technical sense, like Chaucer's *Book of the Duchess*, or Coleridge's own poems: 'The Pains of Sleep' and 'Phantom or Fact'; except in the single detail of the damsel with the dulcimer, that is, it does not purport to relate the experience of a dream. Whether it is 'dream-like' is a matter of definition. For some unexplained reason, that word is commonly applied to the vague, shadowy or mystical, though dreams themselves hardly ever seem to be like this: *Alice in Wonderland*, which is none of these things, surely offers a much more convincing example of what they can be like. Few wide-awake readers will find Lowes's defence of Coleridge's 1816 preface convincing:

> Nobody in his waking senses could have fabricated those amazing eighteen lines [from 'A damsel with a dulcimer . . .']. For if anything ever bore the infallible marks of authenticity, it is that dissolving panorama in which fugitive hints of Aloadine's Paradise succeed each other with the vivid incoherence, and the illusion of natural and expected sequence, and the sense of an identity that yet is not identity, which are the distinctive attributes of dreams.[2]

But it is not at all obvious that the poem is incoherent. In fact it is wonderfully of a piece. Peacock saw this point at once, in an article he drafted in 1818 in reply to the reviewers within two years of its publication. 'There are very few specimens of lyrical poetry,' he argued, 'so plain, so consistent, so completely *simplex et unum* from first to last' as 'Kubla Khan'; and he dismisses the 1816 preface boldly:

> as the story of its having been composed in his sleep must necessarily, by all who are acquainted with his manner of narrating matter of fact, be received with a certain degree of scepticism, its

[2] J. L. Lowes, *The Road to Xanadu*, Boston (1927, revised 1930), p. 363.

value of a psychological curiosity is nothing; and whatever value it has is in its poetic merit alone.[3]

In any case, Coleridge's own views about dreams seem to have been interpretative, more so than Lowes's phrase 'dissolving panorama' would suggest, and he may not have thought 'Kubla Khan' any the less significant or shapely for representing 'a vision in a dream'. Dreams, like poems, seem to have had for him 'a logic of their own':

> Call it a moment's work (and such it seems)
> This tale's a fragment from the life of dreams;
> But say that years matur'd the silent strife,
> And 'tis a record from the dream of life (*CPW* 485).

Dreams have significance, like life itself, and demand interpretation. Certainly 'Kubla Khan' is a difficult poem, in the sense that it calls for careful exegis based on a good deal of information about Coleridge's intellectual preoccupations. But it is not muddled. It may sound faint praise to some to call it one of the best organized of all Coleridge's works: more explicit, perhaps, to remark that it is one of those poems that seem all bones, so firm and self-assertive is the structure. It is not even, on the face of it (to continue the argument as if the troublesome preface did not exist), an emotionally intense poem, apart from the last half-dozen lines. Much of its tone is matter-of-fact, informative, even slightly technical, as if Coleridge was anxious, as he is in the opening section of the 'Mariner', to get his measurements right. And it is worth noticing at once that he does get them right. The reader is enabled and encouraged to construct a model, or draw a map, of the Khan's whole device, and it can be no accident that the figure 'five', mentioned in the sixth line, 'So twice five miles of fertile ground/With walls and towers were girdled round . . .' is repeated in l.25: 'Five miles meandering with a mazy motion . . .'. (This is corrected from 'twice six miles' in the Crewe manuscript.) The walls are ten miles long, in fact, in order to surround the five-mile stretch of the sacred river that is above the

---

[3] 'An Essay on Fashionable Literature', Halliford edition of the *Works of Peacock*, edited by H. F. B. Brett-Smith and C. E. Jones, vol. viii, London (1934), pp. 291, 290.

surface of the earth. Besides, as many have noticed, there seems to be nothing fragmentary about the poem as it survives, in spite of the 1816 subtitle 'A Fragment': it seems to say all it has to say. And the logical progression of the poem is unusually good, each of its four paragraphs being an advance upon its predecessor, and each one tightly organized within itself. All this is not to deny that Coleridge may have composed the poem in a dream, but only to insist that the dream-hypothesis is unhelpful, and even—in so far as it may encourage the reader to let down his guard and disregard what the poem is saying—something of a nuisance.

What is 'Kubla Khan' about? This is, or ought to be, an established fact of criticism: 'Kubla Khan' is a poem about poetry. It is probably the most original poem about poetry in English, and the first hint outside his notebooks and letters that a major critic lies hidden in the twenty-five-year-old Coleridge. Anyone who objects that there is not a word about poetry in it should be sent at once to the conclusion and asked, even if he has never read any Plato, what in English poetry this is like:

> Weave a circle round him thrice,
> And close your eyes with holy dread,
> For he on honey-dew hath fed,
> And drunk the milk of Paradise.

There are dozens of parallels in Renaissance English to this account of poetic inspiration, all based—though rarely at first hand —on Plato's view of poetic madness in the *Ion* or the *Phaedrus*. Shakespeare's banter about 'the poet's eye, is a fine frenzy rolling' in *A Midsummer Night's Dream* is perhaps the most famous. The 'flashing eyes' and 'floating hair' of Coleridge's poem belong to a poet in the fury of creation. Verbal resemblances to the text of Plato itself confirm that the last paragraph of the poem is a prolonged Platonic allusion. Socrates, in the *Ion*, compares lyric poets to 'Bacchic maidens who draw *milk and honey* from the rivers when under the influence of Dionysus' and adds that poets 'gather their strains from *honied fountains* out of the gardens and dells of the Muses. . . .' Ion himself, describing the effects of poetic recitation, confesses that 'when I speak of horrors, my hair stands on end. . . .' The very phrase 'holy dread' is Platonic (*Laws* 671D). That 'Kubla Khan' is in some sense a comment on Plato's theory of poetry is not really in doubt.

Given that 'Kubla Khan' is about poetry, its general direction is not difficult to discern, and real problems only arise in trying to account for detail after detail in terms of its total significance. The fifty-four lines of the poem divide clearly at line 36. The first section, often in coldly literal detail, describes the Khan's 'rare device'. Purchas's *Pilgrimage* (1613) tells us hardly more than that the Khan built a movable palace in a beautifully enclosed park. Coleridge is much more specific, and concentrates many of Purchas's details, and some others, into a closely consistent picture. The park in the poem is a mixture of the natural and the artificial, at once a wilderness and a garden, and what is man-made contains, or is contained in, the wild and uncontrollable:

> And here were forests ancient as the hills
> Enfolding sunny spots of greenery.

Though the whole design is of course artificial—an enclosed park centering upon a palace or 'stately pleasure-dome'—it contains within itself, as its unique possession, something utterly natural and uncontrollable: the sacred river itself, for the rest of its course subterranean, bursts into the light at this point and flows violently above ground before sinking back. It is evidently for this reason that the tyrant chose the site for his palace, which stands so close to the water that it casts its shadow upon it and is within earshot of the sound of the river, both above and below ground. And these two sounds harmonize:

> Where was heard the mingled measure
> From the fountain and the caves.

With full emphasis upon the effect of harmonious contrast, the first section ends.

The second begins on an apparently irrelevant note, but its relevance is justified at once: the song of an Abyssinian girl, once heard in a dream, is capable of moving such 'deep delight' that

> I would build that dome in air . . .

'In air' presumably means not substantially but as a poem, and the reader's first instinct is to say that this is just what Coleridge has done. But this is evidently wrong. The syntax makes it very clear that the project remains unfulfilled:

> And all who heard should see them there,
> And all should cry . . .

'Kubla Khan', then, is not just about poetry: it is about two kinds of poem. One of them is there in the first thirty-six lines of the poem; and though the other is nowhere to be found, we are told what it would do to the reader and what it would do to the poet. The reader would be able to visualize a palace and park he had never seen; and the poet would behave after the classic manner of poets, like a madman. This second poem, a poem that does not exist, is so evidently the real thing that it is clear that the poem of the first thirty-six lines is not—not quite a poem at all, in Coleridge's terms. And if it is asked why Coleridge in 1798 would be likely to find ll.1-36 unpoetical, the question is already answered. They are factual, detailed, matter-of-fact. It is well known precisely why Coleridge objected to 'matter-of-factness' in poetry—the very word, in his view, was his own coinage. In the *Biographia Literaria*, written nearly twenty years later, he lists this quality as the second of Wordsworth's defects as a poet:

> . . . a matter-of-factness in certain poems . . . a laborious minuteness and fidelity in the representation of objects . . . (*BL* xxii).

This may sound rather remote from the twenty-five-year-old poet who wrote 'Kubla Khan'. But Hazlitt, if his evidence is to be trusted (and it may have been conditioned by a reading of this passage in the *Biographia*, which appeared in 1817), supplies the one detail to complete the case. In his essay 'My First Acquaintance with Poets', published in the third number of *The Liberal* (April 1823) he tells how Coleridge had made the same objection to some of Wordsworth's poems in a walk near Nether Stowey in June

1798, only a few weeks after the most probable date of composition of 'Kubla Khan'. Coleridge, says Hazlitt:

> lamented that Wordsworth was not prone enough to believe in the traditional superstitions of the place, and that there was something corporeal, a *matter-of-fact-ness*, a clinging to the palpable, or often to the petty, in his poetry in consequence . . . He said, however (if I remember right) that this objection must be confined to his descriptive pieces, that his philosophic poetry had a grand and comprehensive spirit in it, so that his soul seemed to inhabit the universe like a palace, and to discover truth by intuition rather than by deduction.

Here are two kinds of poetry, and evidence too that this preoccupation of Coleridge's career as a critic was already present in the fertile year of 1797-8. In a sense, it is the same question that led him, in the years that followed, into the period of intense critical activity that began with *The Friend* in 1809 and culminated in the composition of the *Biographia Literaria* in 1815. How far may poetry be purely informative and descriptive? Coleridge's answer, in effect, was 'Ideally, never.' Information is not the characteristic business of poetry. Poetry may have an informative effect, may leave us 'sadder and wiser', as the Mariner's tale left the Wedding Guest. But it ought not to proceed, as some of Wordsworth's lesser poems do, by a mere aggregation of detail (' 'Tis three feet long and two feet wide'). This, on its simplest and most practical level, is the force of Coleridge's imagination/fancy distinction, and there is evidence beyond Hazlitt, in Coleridge's own notebooks and letters, to show how early he hit upon it as a summary of his case for and against Wordsworth's poetry. An early letter of 15 January 1804, addressed to Richard Sharp, contains a full outline of the distinction:

> Imagination, or the *modifying* power in that highest sense of the word, in which I have ventured to oppose it to Fancy, or the *aggregating* power (*CL* ii 1,034).

The interrupted discussion at the end of the thirteenth chapter of the *Biographia Literaria*, where the 'essentially vital' power of imagination is contrasted with the 'fixities and definites' of fancy, fills out the account of a dozen years earlier. But the letter of 1804 is precise enough, and early enough, to make it reasonable to suppose that the young poet of 'Kubla Khan' may already have been close to such a conclusion.

There are two aspects of the imagination/fancy distinction which, obvious as they are, tend perhaps to be overlooked. The first is that it is a value-distinction. 'Imagination' is the power that writes good poems: 'fancy' writes inferior ones. There is no such thing, in Coleridgean terms, as a bad imaginative poem. If the 'shaping spirit' really has shaped, if the poem is more than a sum of its parts and more than a mere aggregate of the poet's perceptions, then it is so far good. Secondly, the distinction is an historical one: it derives from a view of the whole past of English poetry. It is the decisive innovation of the romantic poet to write imaginative poems rather than fanciful ones, just as it was the characteristic role of the Augustans to condemn themselves to a poetry 'addressed to the fancy or the intellect' (*BL* i). Wordsworth, in this view, bestrides both worlds and is pathetically capable of both, and the *Biographia* is a belated plea inviting him to recognize both his excellence and his failings. But it is just here, at this confident moment of exegesis, that an embarrassing choice emerges in the interpretation of 'Kubla Khan'. Given that it is a poem about two kinds of poetry, and that Coleridge's classic distinction may have been present to him, in essence at least, as early as 1798, there is no need to resist the conclusion that its first thirty-six lines are 'fanciful' and the remainder a programme for imaginative creation. But I do not know that there is any clear reason for assigning the fancifulness of the first section of the poem to what Coleridge disliked in the aristocratic poetry of the Augustan era, or to what he disliked in some of Wordsworth's, or to what he disliked in some of his own. The orientalism of the setting of the poem masks, and perhaps deliberately, its critical purpose.

Certainly the Khan is very like a tyrannical aristocrat as seen through romantic and liberal eyes. This is an aspect of the poem that might easily have seemed too obvious, in the years around 1800, to be worth mentioning, but it needs to be emphasized in an

age which finds tyrants engagingly exotic, even to the point supposing Kubla a model of the creative artist. The very fact that he
is an oriental despot would have been reason enough in the late
eighteenth century to excite hostility. To this day the French retain
the word *turquerie* to describe a brutal act. Beckford's *Vathek*
(1786) is one of the many oriental tales of the period, French and
English, that hint at the exotic vices of eastern potentates. And there
is nothing improbable about identifying eighteenth-century aristocratic failings with the medieval or modern East. Cowper vents an
Englishman's indignation in the fifth book of *The Task* (1785)
against Catherine the Great's ingenious Palace of Ice, a 'most magnificent and mighty freak' made without saw or hammer, a 'brittle
prodigy':

>                          a scene
> Of evanescent glory, once a stream
> And soon to slide into a stream again . . .
> 'Twas transient in its nature, as in show
> 'Twas durable: as worthless, as it seem'd
> Intrinsically precious; to the foot
> Treach'rous and false; it smil'd, and it was cold.
>
> Great princes have great playthings . . .
> But war's a game which, were their subjects wise,
> Kings would not play at.

Keats in 'Sleep and Poetry' does not invoke the East to damn
what he supposed the triviality of Augustan poetry; but the language
he uses might be aptly used of the Khan. English poetry between
the Elizabethans and the moderns he sees as a sterile interlude, 'a
schism Nurtured by foppery and barbarism':

>              with a puling infant's force
> They sway'd about upon a rocking horse
> And thought it Pegasus.

The Khan, too, may be something of a barbarous fop. And if
this seems a lofty and remote view of the East, it should be recalled
that accurate orientalism is an extreme rarity in England before the

Victorians; the orientalism of the early Romantics derives from experiences like the childhood reading of the *Arabian Nights* that Wordsworth refers to in the *Prelude* (v. 482f.). It is colourful, picturesque, and indifferent to accuracy, at once fascinated and dismissive. Southey sums up the attitude that Coleridge is likely to have shared in his notes and preface to *Thalaba* (1801), a Moslem tale he began in 1799 in a new metre which was to be 'the *arabesque* ornament of an Arabian tale'. No labour, in Southey's view, could be justified in getting oriental details right. No faithful translation from the Persian could make Firdausi's epic readable, and the *Arabian Nights*, which had first appeared in English in about 1705-8, were all the better for having passed through 'the filter of a French translation'. 'A waste of ornament and labour,' as Southey puts it loftily, 'characterises all the works of the Orientalists'. The East is not an object of study, but a place to let the imagination run riot in. And the chief excitement and source of horror lies in its despotism. Purchas offers rather an attractive picture of the Khan, as well as interesting details about his enormous, if fastidious, sexual appetite; but then Purchas was a Jacobean and took autocracy for granted, and was also impressed by the fact that this Emperor of the Tartars in the 1260's had treated his European guests well and taken a sympathetic interest in Christianity. The sentence from Purchas that Coleridge scribbled in his notebook emphasizes merely his despotism:

> the greatest prince in peoples, cities, and kingdoms that ever was in the world (*CN* 1,840).

The overwhelmingly important fact about the 'pleasure-dome' of the poem, with its surrounding park, is its artificiality. It is a 'miracle of rare device', despotically willed into existence as a tyrant's toy:

> In Xanadu did Kubla Khan
> A stately pleasure-dome decree . . .

The authoritarian word 'decree' is not in Purchas, who simply says: 'In Xaindu did Cublai Can build a stately pallace . . .' And the painfully contrived quality of the tyrant's pleasure becomes clearer with every line: in the formal, though not entirely formal, gardens, and the trivial purpose to which the brute strength of the sacred river has been harnessed. The reader is meant to be left with a disagreeable image of the patron himself, congratulating himself on his facile ingenuity in degrading a matchless natural pheno-menon to the service of a landscape garden—in itself a very Augus-tan pleasure—in order to flatter his own megalomaniac dreams:

> And 'mid this tumult Kubla heard from far
> Ancestral voices prophesying war!

In his artistic tastes, at least, he reminds one a little of the young Alexander Pope's complacent view of Windsor Park:

> Here hills and vales, the woodland and the plain,
> Here earth and water seem to strive again;
> Not Chaos-like together crush'd and bruis'd,
> But, as the world, harmoniously confus'd.
>
> *Windsor-Forest* (1713), ll.11-14

'In perusing French tragedies,' Coleridge remarked years later, 'I have fancied two marks of admiration at the end of each line, as hieroglyphics of the author's own admiration at his own cleverness' (*BL* i). Kubla's arrogance is much like this. If only he knew it, the poem hints, he has bitten off much more than he can chew.

For all the violence of great emotional experience survives there in the river, contained by the Khan's device much as Augustan poems seem to contain and even to sterilize the emotions of man: 'thoughts *translated* into the language of poetry', as Coleridge later complained of Pope. The vast power of the river is allowed to rise, but only 'momently', and then sinks back into silence, 'a lifeless ocean'. This is surely not the River of Life. It is the river of the poetry of imagination which, under the old literary order, had been debased into a plaything and allowed its liberty only if 'girdled round'. The passage that describes the river as it rushes above ground is dense with the imagery of the violent reshaping of dull matter, like the 'essentially vital' power of the imagination working upon objects 'essentially fixed and dead' (*BL* xiii):

> And from this chasm, with ceaseless turmoil seething,
> As if this earth in fast thick pants were breathing,
> A mighty fountain momently was forced,
> Amid whose swift half-intermitted burst
> Huge fragments vaulted like rebounding hail,
> Or chaffy grain beneath the thresher's flail . . .

The poem is profoundly elusive in other ways, but there is something uncharacteristically familiar about Coleridge's imagery here, so commonly are rivers and springs associated with poetry in classical and Renaissance poetry. The very name 'Alph' offers an easy clue in its resemblance to the Alpheus of Milton's 'Lycidas', where it is associated with the Sicilian Muse of pastoral poetry. And the river of poetry was a preoccupation of some Romantics too. In his preface to the sonnets on *The River Duddon* (18nn) Wordsworth was later to urge Coleridge to revive an old project of their Somerset year, a poem describing the course of a symbolic river to be called 'The Brook' (*BL* x). 'There is a sympathy in streams,' as he put it invitingly. The sacred river is the most traditional element in a poem otherwise evasive in its sophistication.

The triumph of 'Kubla Khan', perhaps, lies in its evasions: it hints so delicately at critical truths while demonstrating them so boldly. The contrast between the two halves of the poem, between the terrible emergence of the imaginative power in the first, 'momently forced', and its Dionysiac victory in the second, is bold enough to distract attention from the business at hand. So bold, indeed, that Coleridge for once was able to dispense with any language out of the past. It was his own poem, a manifesto. To read it now, with the hindsight of another age, is to feel premonitions of the critical achievement to come: phrases like 'Poetry is the spontaneous overflow of powerful feelings'[4], or 'the imagination . . . dissolves, diffuses, dissipates, in order to re-create' (*BL* xiii), lie only a little below the surface of the poem. But the poem is in advance, not just of these, but in all probability of any critical statement that survives. It may be that it stands close to the moment of discovery itself.

[4] Wordsworth's preface to *Lyrical Ballads* (1800), an essay in some degree a work of collaboration between the two poets.

CHAPTER NINE

# The Last Poems

If Wordsworth and Coleridge had died before middle age, as Byron, Shelley and Keats did, much profitless speculation as well as much good poetry would have been lost. It is profitless, certainly, in the face of so much that is excellent, to debate about 'what went wrong'. In Coleridge's case a good deal went right, and poems as notable as 'The Delinquent Travellers', 'Work without Hope' and 'The Garden of Boccaccio' survive to astonish anyone taught to believe that Coleridge ceased to be a poet after the Dejection Ode of 1802. What rather happened was that, at the age of thirty, he ceased to be a prolific poet and became an occasional one. The matter of bulk establishes the point quickly. If the dramas are excluded, only about a quarter of Coleridge's verse was written after the age of thirty. A flood turns into a trickle. But the spring never dries up. The possibility, and even the fact, of excellence remains, poetic projects abound and are often fulfilled, and until his death in 1834 Coleridge remained by choice a literary man rather than a philosopher, a sage, or a mere invalid in retirement. It is true, of course, that he was a philosopher, sage and invalid too; but he chose to play all three roles, so to say, in literary dress. It is remarkable how much of his thinking to the end was conducted in verse. In spite of the prose tracts of the last nine years, beginning with *Aids to Reflection* (1825), Coleridge remained for his contemporaries primarily a great poet. His wider influence as a religious and political thinker, which was promoted by the posthumous publication of his *Table Talk* (1835), *Literary Remains* (1836-9) and other papers, and by John Stuart Mill's salute to him as a seminal mind in the *Westminster Review* of 1840, is essentially a Victorian phenomenon. Leigh Hunt, who was only a dozen years younger, half dismisses what he calls 'the *prose* part' of Coleridge's mind in his anthology *Imagination and Fancy* (1844), and then asserts:

> Of pure poetry, strictly so called, that is to say, consisting of nothing but its essential self, without conventional and perishing helps, he was the greatest master of his time. If you could see it in a phial, like a distillation of roses, . . . it would be found without a speck (p. 250).

That was written ten years after Coleridge's death, but it is very much the view of a contemporary, and it sets the tone of Regency comment. Thomas Barnes of the *Times*, in an anonymous article in *The Champion* thirty years before, had made the point even more searchingly, though more effusively too:

> the man whose every metaphor and illustration is a poetic image, whose metaphysics are led through the flowers of fancy instead of the intricacies of reason, and whose diction aims at all the gorgeous array and musical pomp of the most stately verse. . . .[1]

The great theme of the last poems, first fully stated in the Dejection Ode of 1802, is unrequited love. 'The Blossoming of the Solitary Date-Tree', a poem of 1805, sums up in its very title the paradox of a creativity of despair. 'Why was I made for Love and Love denied to me?' (*CPW* 397), the question on which the poem ends, is posed and left unanswered again and again over the next thirty years. It would be rash, all the same, to conclude that Coleridge's activity as a poet diminished because Sara Hutchinson refused him. A fall of poetic temperature is so general a fact among romantic poets that only a general answer will do. To ignore, for a moment, the differences between poems as exactly contemporaneous as 'The Ancient Mariner' and 'Tintern Abbey', or between the Dejection Ode and Immortality, the outline of an answer may present itself in these terms. The first pair of poems (if my account of the 'Mariner' is accepted) treat the loss-and-gain of growing up.

---

[1] 'Mr Coleridge', *The Champion* (27 March 1814), under Barnes's pseudonym 'Strada'. I am indebted to Mr Donald Low of Pembroke College, Cambridge, for this reference.

The second pair, from a vantage-point four or five years onwards, offer a less vivid but conceptually fuller description of what such loss can mean—'a grief without a pang'. If this concern lay at the root of the productive years of 1797-1802, it is not surprising if the creativity of Wordsworth and Coleridge diminished in later life. The subject of their major poems is a period of transition in early manhood, when some vital part of our instinctual life is forever lost. To make poetry of such a loss, the poet needs an immediate consciousness of what once was as much as an awareness of his present state. A faint memory is hardly enough. This is perhaps the nature of the arctic summer of inspiration in the first Romantics. It is a fact of Wordsworth's career as well as of Coleridge's, after all, and demands no external agency like opium or unrequited love. Coleridge made the point in one of his 1818 lectures so explicitly that it is a wonder anyone has ever been misled into false biographical inferences:

> Remark the seeming identity of body and mind in infants, and thence the loveliness of the former; the commencing separation in boyhood, and the struggle of equilibrium in youth: thence onward the body is first simply indifferent; then demanding the translucency of the mind not to be worse than indifferent; and finally all that presents the body as body becoming almost of an excremental nature.[2]

In any case, by 1802 the task was accomplished. The problem of discovering an audience for romantic poetry, which had seemed almost hopeless less than ten years before, had been found a provisional solution in the conversation poem addressed to a single friend; and Wordsworth was to consolidate this solution so successfully that by 1850, when the *Prelude* first appeared, the address to Coleridge on which the poem closes seems little more than an exquisite superfluity. The *Prelude* really speaks to all manner of men; the problem has ceased to be a problem. More than that, the fertility of Coleridge's mastery of poetic languages and metrical experiments was already by 1802 a wonder of the age. Byron and

[2] *Literary Remains*, edited by H. N. Coleridge, London (1836-9), vol. i, p. 230.

Scott did not wait to see 'Christabel' published or even finished before imitating it; Keats's 'Eve of St Agnes' owes enormously, in detail and in manner, to Coleridge's experiments in the medieval; and in Shelley the lesson of infinite poetic imitation, without limit as to place and time, has been learned with a vengeance. Coleridge's immediate circle, and especially the Wordsworths, may have thought him something of a disappointment, but the literary world decidedly did not. The earlier, and more notorious reviews of Coleridge's poems, such as the damnation of 'Christabel' in the *Edinburgh Review* (September 1816) once thought to be by Hazlitt, do not justly represent his reputation during his later life as the Sage of Highgate (1816-34); they are rude interruptions in a fairly even tenor of hero-worship. This is not surprising, since in Coleridge nineteenth-century poetry was to find much of its doctrine and example. The example has been the subject of this book: the doctrine of the 'symbolical' came through slowly, muddily, and remains to this day subject to dispute, open to the charge of plagiarism from contemporary German metaphysicians. But even for the young Coleridge it was the ultimate poetic solution, as the early poems show, and his successor-poets of the nineteenth and twentieth centuries have tended to agree with him. Symbol is, for the modern poet, the point at which the poem finds repose and form. 'Real is to symbolical as motion is to rest at the goal' (*CN* 2,530), as he wrote in 1805 in the form of a mathematical equation; and, shortly after, 'I seem rather to be seeking, as it were *asking*, a symbolical language for something within me that already and forever exists, than observing any thing new' (*CN* 2,546). These gropings towards an explanation of the new kind of poem he has already made touched something fairly explicit, a decade later, in his account of the symbol in the *Statesman's Manual* (1816): it 'always partakes of the reality which it renders intelligible; and while it enunciates the whole, abides itself as a living part in that unity of which it is the representative' (pp. 36-7). The doctrine is illuminating, but it remains less solid and less original than the example; informative, but less informative than the Mariner's albatross or the figure of Geraldine.

The 'Hymn before Sun-Rise, in the Vale of Chamouni', a poem

written a few months after the Dejection Ode (August-September 1802), seems to be openly offered as an example and a test of the symbolical. 'The mood and habit of mind out of which the Hymn rose,' as he wrote in a letter of 1819, was deliberately different from that of Milton, Thomson or the Psalmist in its response to the individual object: 'From my very childhood I have been accustomed to abstract and, as it were, unrealize whatever of more than common interest my eyes dwelt on, and then by a sort of transfusion and transmission of my consciousness to identify myself with the object . . . If ever I should feel once again the genial warmth and stir of the poetic impulse . . . I should venture on a yet stranger and wilder allegory of yore . . . I would allegorize myself as a rock' (*CL* iv 974-5). The poem belongs to the most characteristic of all Coleridgean forms, the 'introversive reflection' (*CN* 3,270) by which some given original is used for the purpose of self-discovery and self-revelation. But something almost perverse seems to be at work in the Hymn. No one would ever guess from the poem itself, or from the notes that Coleridge attached to it, that it is a translation, expanded to four times the original length, of a German poem by the Swiss poetess Friederika Brun; and no one would guess that Coleridge, who had climbed Scafell in August 1802, had never seen the valley in Savoy in which the poem is set. The source was not pointed out until a few weeks after Coleridge's death, by De Quincey in *Tait's Magazine* (September 1834); though in demonstrating the innocent plagiarism De Quincey also insisted that Coleridge had awakened 'the dry bones of the German outline . . . into the fulness of life'. Even the German prose notes that accompany the poem in Frau Brun's *Gedichte* (Zürich, 1795) have been used in the Hymn itself or in its accompanying notes. Coleridge's failure to declare his source, in this case, seems merely pointless: much of the point of an imitation is lost, after all, if knowledge of the original is lost. The German poem is a brief, rapturous *Sturm-und-Drang* ode addressed to Klopstock, its manner a little too close to Coleridge's old exclamatory style of the mid-1790's to be a happy assumption for him in middle life. And the image of the poet as a mountain, with its dark base and bright summit, suffers from an obviousness that is foreign to the romantic symbol:

> Oft from whose feet the avalanche, unheard,
> Shoots downward, glittering through the pure serene
> Into the depth of clouds that veil thy breast . . . (*CPW* 380).

The paradox of strife co-existing with harmony and rest in the glaciers or 'silent cataracts' of the mountain echoes the paradox of Kubla Khan's pleasure-dome, and suffers from the comparison too.

The scattered excellences of the last thirty years of Coleridge's life can only be suggested here. These poems are largely unknown, and some of them have suffered fates stranger than neglect: 'Ne Plus Ultra', for example, an ode apparently addressed to the Devil, was once attributed to Isaac Rosenberg.[3] Many explore the human paradox of creative despair—the 'positive Negation' of man, as he calls it in 'Limbo' (*CPW* 431)—which may be the best that life offers, since man is himself a walking paradox:

> Thou hast no reason why! Thou canst have none;
> Thy being's being is contradiction (*CPW* 426).

In 'Self-Knowledge', one of the very last of his poems, the metre and manner of Pope's *Essay on Man* ('Know then thyself . . .') are parodied, a contradiction of style used to assert a contradiction of sense:

> What has thou, Man, that thou dar'st call thine own?—
> What is there in thee, Man, that can be known?—
> Dark fluxion, all unfixable by thought,
> A phantom dim of past and future wrought (*CPW* 487).

Other poems are surprising even for Coleridge. 'The Delinquent Travellers', a brief Byronic satire against tourism written in 1824, the year of Byron's death, was not published until the present century (*CPW* 443), and is in rhyming four-footers that turn their back on the subtle fluidity of 'Christabel' in favour of a bouncing comic vigour. The poem seems to have been provoked, like others among the later poems, not by an historical recollection like the Middle Ages or the Metaphysical poets, but rather by something

---

[3] Rosenberg, *Collected Works*, London (1937), p. 119; *CPW* 431.

arrestingly topical that had chanced to fall under his eye a moment before writing the poem. Captain George Lyon's *Private Journal* (1824), an account of an arctic sojourn among the Esquimaux of northern Canada during a vain search for the Northwest Passage, was just the sort of book to take Coleridge's fancy; the very frontispiece, which shows an icebound ship turned into a kind of house, is forbiddingly entitled 'The Last Appearance of the Sun for 42 Days', and may have reminded him of his own Mariner at another Pole. Coleridge uses the journal not for any organic purpose, but merely as he had used the quotation from the 'Ballad of Sir Patrick Spence' at the beginning of the Dejection Ode, more than twenty years before, to give himself an easy entry, at once colloquial and ironic, into the poem itself:

> Some are home-sick—some two or three,
> Their third year on the Arctic Sea—
> Brave Captain Lyon tells us so—
> Spite of those charming Esquimaux.
> But O, what scores are sick of home,
> Agog for Paris or for Rome! . . .

The poem is his only Byronic imitation—a poem satirizing tourism in the manner of the greatest tourist of the age. It occasionally exploits the technique of the deliberately bad rhyme that Byron had popularized in *Don Juan*:

> If you but perch, where Dover tallies
> So strangely with the coast of Calais,

though the real Byronism of the poem lies in its characteristic tone of affectionate iconoclasm, a kind of cosmic banter that should help to dispel the myth of Coleridge's unending solemnity:

> Move, or be moved—there's no protection,
> Our Mother Earth has ta'en the infection—
> (That rogue Copernicus, 'tis said,
> First put the whirring in her head)
> A planet she, and can't endure
> T'exist without her annual tour:

> The *name* were else a mere misnomer,
> Since Planet is but Greek for *Roamer*.

A few months later, in February 1825, 'Work without Hope' was written as if to confirm the variety of his gifts. The poem is a brief, pathetic and shapely footnote to the Dejection Ode—the more shapely for the loss of a personal passage which in the notebook concludes the poem (*CPW* 1,110-1). The notebook is unhelpful in other ways. Coleridge there calls the poem a 'Strain in the Manner of George Herbert', which it certainly is not, though its opening,

> All Nature seems at work. Slugs leave their lair—
> The bees are stirring—birds are on the wing (*CPW* 447),

is presumed an echo of the last stanza of the first of Herbert's poems entitled 'Praise':

> O raise me then! Poor bees, that work all day,
>   Sting my delay,
> Who have a work, as well as they,
>   And much, much more.

But 'Work without Hope' is in no sense an imitation of *The Temple*, which supplies nothing but its initial impetus. It is a brief exercise in the old and unforgotten manner of the conversation poem, now aptly addressed to no one in particular:

> Work without Hope draws nectar in a sieve,
> And Hope without an object cannot live.

The notebook also invites belief that the poem refers to the twenty-ninth chapter of Genesis, and that it is addressed by Jacob to Rachel in the tenth year of his service, when 'he saw in her, or fancied that he saw, symptoms of alienation'. The pretence of impersonality seems too thin to be useful, and it is not surprising if Coleridge never published his introduction to the poem.

The haunting knowledge that love was forever lost lies behind 'The Improvisatore' of 1827, a thin little work in execution, and yet one that remains powerfully symptomatic, especially in its title,

138

of Coleridge's consciousness of the nature of his own gifts. It was perhaps provoked by an undergraduate collection of verse *The Improvisatore* (1821) by Thomas Lovell Beddoes, the son of one of his closest friends—Gothic poems which themselves owe something to 'Christabel' and 'The Eve of St Agnes'. But Byron too, both in *Beppo* (1818) and in the fifteenth canto of *Don Juan* (1824), had invoked the colourful Italian profession of one who recites extempore verses to order as a party entertainer. The work begins as a prose dialogue between two young ladies, soon joined by the Improvisatore, an elderly gentleman who obviously represents Coleridge himself. At their request he quotes from a song of Thomas Moore and from Beaumont and Fletcher's *The Elder Brother*, adapting a passage of prose from the play into barely passable Jacobean blank verse; and finally improvises an original poem in praise of marriage. The one memorable aspect of the work, which taken as a whole is a piece of the purest self-indulgence, lies in the prose self-portrait, where the Improvisatore describes his own failure as a husband in terms that provide a moment of piercing self-revelation: 'For some mighty good sort of people, too, there is not seldom a sort of solemn saturnine or, if you will, ursine vanity, that keeps itself alive by sucking the paws of its own self-importance' (*CPW* 465).

The best of the later poems, 'The Garden of Boccaccio' of 1828, comprises in loose nostalgic vein the greater part of Coleridge's fifty years as a poet. It ought to be better known; it ought, in fact, to be the poem first turned to, after the conversation poems, the 'Mariner', 'Kubla Khan' and 'Christabel', to confirm the stature of his poetic art. If it were not for the most part in the very uncharacteristic metre of heroic couplets, and if it were not addressed to a picture rather than to a person, one would have no hesitation in calling it the last of Coleridge's conversation poems. The description remains helpful and almost accurate. The 'Garden' moves in the same alternating pattern between the particular and the general, between the domestic and the visionary, like 'The Eolian Harp', 'Frost at Midnight' or the Dejection Ode; it uses as a point of entry a mere domestic detail—in this case, Mrs Gillman's placing on the poet's desk, to relieve his melancholy, an 'exquisite design' by the contemporary painter and engraver Thomas Stothard (1755-

1834) illustrating Boccaccio's First Day for a London edition of the *Decamerone* (1825); and it uses the event, as weather is used at the beginning of the Dejection Ode, as a point of rapid take-off. By the end of the first paragraph melancholy is cured, and the engraving is already

> An idyll, with Boccaccio's spirit warm,
> Framed in the silent poesy of form (*CPW* 478).

By the second paragraph the total movement of the poem is emergent: the engraving reminds the poet not just of his 'selfless boyhood' as a reader of poetry, or of a visit to Tuscany twenty-two years before, or of the European past that literature has let him live in, but of his total debt to Europe down the years. It is a debt to vitality and variety from one who had always sought not one model but many, from a spirit that 'loved ere it loved, and sought a form for love':

> Wild strains of Scalds, that in the sea-worn caves
> Rehearsed their war-spell to the winds and waves;
> Or fateful hymn of those prophetic maids
> That call'd on Hertha in deep forest glades;
> Or minstrel lay that cheer'd the baron's feast;
> Or rhyme of city pomp, of monk and priest,
> Judge, mayor, and many a guild in long array,
> To high-church pacing on the great saint's day . . .

By this time the 'call on the past' is not a matter of solace, as first it seemed, but of celebration; and the poet, now 'all awake' and his dejection forgotten, is at liberty to 'wander through the Eden' of Stothard's picture. It is at this point that the ultimate Coleridgean device is used: the poet passes into the looking-glass and out the other side. As in the last paragraph of 'Kubla Khan', he ceases to describe and begins to live:

> I see no longer! I myself am there,
> Sit on the ground-sward, and the banquet share . . .
> The brightness of the world, O thou once free,
> And always fair, rare land of courtesy!

> O Florence! with the Tuscan fields and hills,
> And famous Arno, fed with all their rills;
> Thou brightest star of star-bright Italy!
> Rich, ornate, populous—all treasures thine,
> The golden corn, the olive, and the vine . . .

This ecstatic image of Italy, with its Palladian palaces, fountains, gardens, flowers and marble urns, bears about the same remote relation to Stothard's engraving as 'Kubla Khan' to a passage from Purchas. The picture sketched in the climax of the poem is a picture that does not exist; it lives only in the poet's 'inward sight' (l. 24), and it lives there to record lovingly a multiple literary debt:

> See! Boccacce sits, unfolding on his knees
> The new-found roll of old Maeonides;
> But from his mantle's fold, and near the heart,
> Peers Ovid's holy book of Love's sweet smart!
> O all-enjoying and all-blending sage . . .

'All-enjoying and all-blending' is the right note of conclusion. The words would make a fitter epitaph than the pathetic lines Coleridge wrote for himself a few months before his death in July 1834, for the grave where

> A poet lies, or that which once seem'd he (*CPW* 492).

Modesty alone would forbid it; but among the fittest of epitaphs might be the lines which, out of the generosity of his heart, he had written for Wordsworth a quarter of a century before, in 1807, on those poets who

> Have all one age, and from one visible space
> Shed influence. They, both in power and act,
> Are permanent, and Time is not with them,
> Save as it worketh for them, they in it (*CPW* 406).

This offers something like a full measure of Coleridge's originality. He let time work for the poet, and for half a century he worked as a poet in it, annexing the past to his art as no English poet had done before him. Such annexations, at this distance, have acquired a striking air of permanence. The large progression of the ages from the neoclassical imitation to modern symbol has already, in all likelihood, proved too rich in possibilities ever to be reversed. Pure contemporaneity, or even contentment with a single past like ancient Rome, would now seem a precarious affectation, and English poetry seems likely to remain forever various in the languages at its command. The most natural fact of its existence lies in its abundance of forms and of languages: it knows too many times and places ever again to be content with one.

# Index

'Christabel', x, 12, 68, 85, 86, 99, 105-
15, 117-18, 136, 139; Ruskin on, 18;
reviewed, 134
Christ's Hospital, 10n., 11, 47, 48
Cicero, 19
Clare, John, 29
Clarke, M. L., 22n.
Coburn, Kathleen, x, 5n.
Coleorton, 80
Coleridge, Edith, 107n.
Coleridge, E. H., x
Coleridge, Hartley, 70, 72-3, 106
Coleridge, H. N., 35n., 94, 111, 133n.
Coleridge, Mr Justice, 107
Coleridge, Sara (Mrs S. T. Coleridge),
65-6
Coleridge, Sara (Mrs H. N. Coleridge),
3, 107
Collins, William, 51, 52
Columbus, 89
'Constancy to an Ideal Object', 100
conversation poems, 49, 61-84, 138, 139-
40
Corneille, Pierre, 54
Cottle, Joseph, 40
Cowley, Abraham, 19, 20, 22
Cowper, William, 14, 33, 42, 51, 61,
63f., 82, 108, 127
Crane, R. S., 20n.
Crashaw, Richard, 109
Crewe MS, 119, 121
Cudworth, Ralph, 92
Culbone, 119

Dante Alighieri, 26, 39
Darwin, Erasmus, 41, 52
Davie, Donald, 82
Dejection Ode, 9, 50, 73-80, 101, 103,
131, 132, 135, 137, 139, 140
'Delinquent Travellers', 131, 136-8
Denham, Sir John, 20
De Quincey, Thomas, 30-1, 56, 98, 135
'Destiny of Nations', 51, 52
'Devonshire Roads', 48
Donne, John, 4
Drake, Sir Francis, 90
drama, 53-9

dreams, 119f.
Dryden, John, ix, 42, 54; on imitation,
19f.; *Absalom and Achitophel,* 14
Dyer, John, 49

'Easter Holidays', 47
effusions, 49f.
Eliot, T. S., ix, 4, 15, 17, 37
Empson, William, 18
'Eolian Harp', 61, 63, 64, 65-7, 70, 72n.,
108, 139
epic, 14-15, 34
'Epitaph', 100, 141
Erasmus, 19
Euclid, 48

*Fall of Robespierre,* 54-5
fancy, 125f.
'Fears in Solitude', 71
Firdausi, 128
Fletcher, John, 139
fragments, 12-13, 122
'France: an Ode', 42, 50
'Frost at Midnight', 42, 49, 70-1, 74,
83, 117, 139
Frye, Northrop, 15-16

'Garden of Boccaccio', 9, 131, 139-41
German, knowledge of, 55-6, 108
Gillman, James, 10, 107
Gillman, Mrs, 139
Glycine's song, 73
Goethe, J. W. von, 14, 26, 27, 56
Gothic novel, 28, 40, 110-15
Gothic, the, 24, 39-40, 139
Gradus, 22, 23
Gray, Thomas, 22, 50, 51, 52, 82
Greville, Fulke, 42
Griggs, E. L., x
Gutch notebook, 97

Hakluyt, Richard, 118
Hayley, William, 41
Hazlitt, William, 64n.; a 'loveless
observer', 7; on Romantics, 29-30; on
'matter-of-fact', 124-5; and 'Christabel', 134